1st EDITION

Perspectives on Modern World History

The Oklahoma City Bombing

1st EDITION

Perspectives on Modern World History

The Oklahoma City Bombing

Diane Andrews Henningfeld

Editor

GREENHAVEN PRESS
A part of Gale, Cengage Learning

GALE
CENGAGE Learning

Detroit • New York • San Francisco • New Haven, Conn • Waterville, Maine • London

Elizabeth Des Chenes, *Managing Editor*

© 2012 Greenhaven Press, a part of Gale, Cengage Learning.

Gale and Greenhaven Press are registered trademarks used herein under license.

For more information, contact:
Greenhaven Press
27500 Drake Rd.
Farmington Hills, MI 48331-3535
Or you can visit our Internet site at gale.cengage.com.

For product information and technology assistance, contact us at
Gale Customer Support, 1-800-877-4253.

For permission to use material from this text or product, submit all requests online at
www.cengage.com/permissions.

Further permissions questions can be e-mailed to permissionrequest@cengage.com.

Articles in Greenhaven Press anthologies are often edited for length to meet page requirements. In addition, original titles of these works are changed to clearly present the main thesis and to explicitly indicate the author's opinion. Every effort is made to ensure that Greenhaven Press accurately reflects the original intent of the authors. Every effort has been made to trace the owners of copyrighted material.

Cover images © Ralf-Finn Hestoff/Corbis and © imac/Alamy.

LIBRARY OF CONGRESS CATALOGING-IN-PUBLICATION DATA

The Oklahoma City Bombing / Diane Andrews Henningfeld, book editor.
    p. cm. -- (Perspectives on modern world history)
    Includes bibliographical references and indexes.
ISBN 978-0-7377-5796-5 (hardcover)
1. Oklahoma City Federal Building Bombing, Oklahoma City, Okla., 1995. 2. Bombings--Oklahoma --Oklahoma City--History--20th century. 3. Domestic terrorism--Oklahoma--Oklahoma City --History--20th century. I. Henningfeld, Diane Andrews.
    HV6432.6.O345 2012
    363.32509766'38--dc23   2011038118

Printed in the United States of America
1 2 3 4 5 6 7 16 15 14 13 12

CONTENTS

victims of the Oklahoma City bombing. He speaks of the sacrifices made by them and their families, and also of the strength demonstrated by the survivors.

CHAPTER 2

Controversies Surrounding the Oklahoma City Bombing

An attorney states that McVeigh's confessions made to reporters were not true. He contends that the government did not want to reveal the truth of their investigation, and that McVeigh craved the limelight the confession brought him.

Doe No. 2 never existed. Defense lawyers for McVeigh disagree with their client's assertion.

In 2011, a so-called homeless man was arrested in Quincy, Massachusetts; he turned out to be a person of interest in the Oklahoma City bombing. A private investigator claims that this man, Hussain Hashem al-Hussaini, is John Doe No. 2, McVeigh's purported collaborator.

A novelist and former diplomat writes that Terry Nichols's membership in the Michigan militia resulted in the press smearing the nationwide militia movement. He rejects the media's characterizations and claims that militia members do not hate the government and just want to be ready in the event of a national emergency.

A civil rights activist argues that the Oklahoma City bombing alerted Americans to the danger presented by right-wing extremist militia groups and that there has been a resurgence of such groups "who are already armed and preparing for potential conflict with the government."

CHAPTER 3   Personal Narratives

FOREWORD

"History cannot give us a program for the future, but it can give us a fuller understanding of ourselves, and of our common humanity, so that we can better face the future."

—Robert Penn Warren,
American poet and novelist

The history of each nation is punctuated by momentous events that represent turning points for that nation, with an impact felt far beyond its borders. These events—displaying the full range of human capabilities, from violence, greed, and ignorance to heroism, courage, and strength—are nearly always complicated and multifaceted. Any student of history faces the challenge of grasping the many strands that constitute such world-changing events as wars, social movements, and environmental disasters. But understanding these significant historic events can be enhanced by exposure to a variety of perspectives, whether of people involved intimately or of ones observing from a distance of miles or years. Understanding can also be increased by learning about the controversies surrounding such events and exploring hot-button issues from multiple angles. Finally, true understanding of important historic events involves knowledge of the events' human impact—of the ways such events affected people in their everyday lives—all over the world.

Perspectives on Modern World History examines global historic events from the twentieth-century onward by presenting analysis and observation from numerous vantage points. Each volume offers high school, early college level, and general interest readers a thematically arranged anthology of previously published materials that address a major historical event, with an emphasis on international coverage. Each volume opens with background information on the event, then presents the controversies surrounding that event, and concludes with first-person narratives from people who lived through the event or were affected by it. By providing primary sources from the time of the event, as well as relevant commentary surrounding the event, this series can be used to inform debate, help develop critical thinking skills, increase global awareness, and enhance an understanding of international perspectives on history.

Material in each volume is selected from a diverse range of sources, including journals, magazines, newspapers, nonfiction books, personal narratives, speeches, congressional testimony, government documents, pamphlets, organization newsletters, and position papers. Articles taken from these sources are carefully edited and introduced to provide context and background. Each volume of Perspectives on Modern World History includes an array of views on events of global significance. Much of the material comes from international sources and from US sources that provide extensive international coverage.

Each volume in the Perspectives on Modern World History series also includes:

- A full-color **world map**, offering context and geographic perspective.
- An annotated **table of contents** that provides a brief summary of each essay in the volume.
- An **introduction** specific to the volume topic.
- For each viewpoint, a brief **introduction** that has notes about the author and source of the viewpoint, and that provides a summary of its main points.
- Full-color **charts**, **graphs**, **maps**, and other visual representations.

- Informational **sidebars** that explore the lives of key individuals, give background on historical events, or explain scientific or technical concepts.
- A **glossary** that defines key terms, as needed.
- A **chronology** of important dates preceding, during, and immediately following the event.
- A **bibliography** of additional books, periodicals, and websites for further research.
- A comprehensive **subject index** that offers access to people, places, and events cited in the text.

Perspectives on Modern World History is designed for a broad spectrum of readers who want to learn more about not only history but also current events, political science, government, international relations, and sociology—students doing research for class assignments or debates, teachers and faculty seeking to supplement course materials, and others wanting to improve their understanding of history. Each volume of Perspectives on Modern World History is designed to illuminate a complicated event, to spark debate, and to show the human perspective behind the world's most significant happenings of recent decades.

INTRODUCTION

On April 19, 1995, just before 9:00 A.M., Timothy McVeigh parked a Ryder rental truck loaded with explosives in front of the Alfred P. Murrah Federal Building in Oklahoma City, Oklahoma, and walked away. At 9:02 A.M., the truck exploded, ripping apart the Murrah Building and others in the vicinity. The explosion killed 168 people and injured more than 500 others. Many of the dead and injured were children.

At the time, the Oklahoma City bombing was the worst terrorist attack on US soil. It was not, however, the first such attack.

The US Department of State in their publication *Patterns of Global Terrorism* (2001) uses the definition of terrorism found in Title 22 of the United States Code, Section 2656f(d): "The term 'terrorism' means premeditated, politically motivated violence perpetrated against noncombatant targets by subnational groups or clandestine agents, usually intended to influence an audience." This definition succinctly summarizes the key characteristics of terrorism.

Under this definition, there are those who would argue that the famous Boston Tea Party of 1773 was an act of economic terrorism: the so-called "Sons of Liberty"—a subnational, clandestine group—committed sabotage against property belonging to the noncombatant British East India Company in protest to a hated tax levied by the British government. They intended to influence the British to repeal the tax and to catalyze other colonists to join the independence movement. Clearly, most Americans view the Boston Tea Party as a patriotic statement against tyranny. Yet the actions of the colonists could be viewed in a different light.

Nearly one hundred years later, in the aftermath of the American Civil War, clandestine organizations such as the Ku Klux Klan waged war against those who were neither white nor Protestant. Their actions were premeditated and violent, and perpetrated against noncombatants. Many of their actions resulted in the deaths of African Americans and other minorities, through arson and lynching. According to journalist Bill Moyers, "Alabama's Tuskegee Institute maintained statistics on lynchings in America from 1882 to 1968. Their total: 4,749."

Domestic terrorism continued into the twentieth century. In 1920, in an incident that eerily foreshadows McVeigh's movements, Wall Street was the target of a terrorist attack. According to the Federal Bureau of Investigation:

> A non-descript man driving a cart pressed an old horse forward on a mid-September day in 1920. He stopped the animal and its heavy load in front of the U.S. Assay Office, across from the J.P. Morgan building in the heart of Wall Street. The driver got down and quickly disappeared into the crowd.

The cart exploded, sending shards of metal into the lunch-hour throngs. Thirty people were killed immediately and more than three hundred were injured, many of them dying later in the day. The FBI investigated but could not find the perpetrator. Eventually, the Wall Street bombing was attributed to a left-wing anarchist group.

Likewise, the 1960s, 1970s, and 1980s were rife with politically motivated civil violence. Thus, Timothy McVeigh's actions cannot be seen as an isolated incident in US history, although it was a particularly brutal and costly one.

McVeigh's actions also had personal motivation, and his path to Oklahoma City started long before April 19, 1995. Most biographers point to McVeigh's childhood and his fascination with guns and the survivalist movement as the first steps down this road.

McVeigh's tenure in the US Army was another turning point. His early years in the service were a high point in his life; he was an outstanding gunner and served with distinction during the Persian Gulf War in 1991. After returning to the United States, McVeigh was accepted for training in the army's Special Forces unit. However, McVeigh withdrew from the course when his performance fell below his personal standard. Significantly, about this time he grew increasingly disenchanted with the US government.

It is difficult to say, nonetheless, if McVeigh would have continued down the path to terrorism but for two events. In 1992, federal agents laid siege to survivalist Randy Weaver's compound in rural Ruby Ridge, Idaho, to arrest him on a bench warrant for failing to appear in court. By the time the siege was over, Weaver's son, wife, and a deputy US marshal were dead. McVeigh was incensed at the government's conduct in this situation.

The second event was Waco. On February 28, 1993, agents of the US Bureau of Alcohol, Tobacco and Firearms attempted to serve a search and arrest warrant on David Koresh and members of the Branch Davidian religious community living in the Mt. Carmel compound near the city of Waco, Texas. In the process, six Branch Davidians and four federal agents were killed, initiating a fifty-one-day standoff. On April 19, 1993, federal agents stormed the compound, using tanks and gas. In the resulting conflagration, seventy-four men, women, and children were killed.

McVeigh believed the government murdered these people, according to Lou Michel and Dan Herbeck in *American Terrorist: Timothy McVeigh and the Oklahoma City Bombing* (2001). Slowly, the idea that he needed to make a violent, public statement grew in McVeigh's mind, an idea he developed with the help of his friends Terry Nichols and Michael Fortier. He decided he would avenge the dead of Waco through his destruction of the

Alfred P. Murrah Federal Building in Oklahoma City on the second anniversary of Waco. On tapes recorded by Michel and Herbeck, McVeigh stated, "With Oklahoma City being a counterattack, I was only fighting by the rules of engagement that were introduced by the aggressor. Waco started this war. Hopefully, Oklahoma City would end it."

McVeigh thought of himself as a patriot, not a terrorist. McVeigh blew up the Murrah Building not only as an act of revenge but also as a clarion call to concerned citizens that the government was bent on destroying their liberty. McVeigh was executed for his crime on June 11, 2001, without any expression of remorse or apology.

To the end, McVeigh identified himself with the patriots of the American Revolution. He told Michel and Herbeck:

> I bombed the Murrah Building. . . . I like the phrase "shot heard 'round the world," and I don't think there's any doubt that the Oklahoma City blast was heard around the world. . . . I have great respect for human life. My decision to take human life at the Murrah Building—I did not do it for personal gain. . . . I did it for the larger good.

McVeigh was not alone in his hatred for the US government, and in the years since the Oklahoma City bombing, that hatred has become evident once again. On August 12, 2009, the Southern Poverty Law Center (SPLC), a nonprofit civil rights organization that tracks hate groups and crimes across the nation, reported that the militia movement, "infused with racism," has made a startling resurgence since the election of President Barack Obama in 2008. The SPLC writes:

> Almost a decade after virtually disappearing from public view, the antigovernment militia movement is surging across the country, fueled by fears of a black man in

the White House, the changing demographics of the country, and conspiracy theories increasingly spread by mainstream figures.

Further, Peter Grier, writing in the April 19, 2010, issue of the *Christian Science Monitor*, agrees with former President Bill Clinton that on the fifteenth anniversary of the Oklahoma City bombing, the "political environment of today has some dangerous similarities to that of 1995."

Will the current political environment lead an American to inflict violence on fellow citizens with the terror of something like the Oklahoma City bombing? That would be impossible to predict. In the words of Homeland Security secretary Janet Napolitano, speaking on April 19, 2010, at the Oklahoma City Memorial, "Terrorism is a tactic not just to kill, but to make us feel powerless. But we are never powerless. We control the way we prepare ourselves, the way we anticipate and combat the threats, and the way we respond if something does happen."

World Map

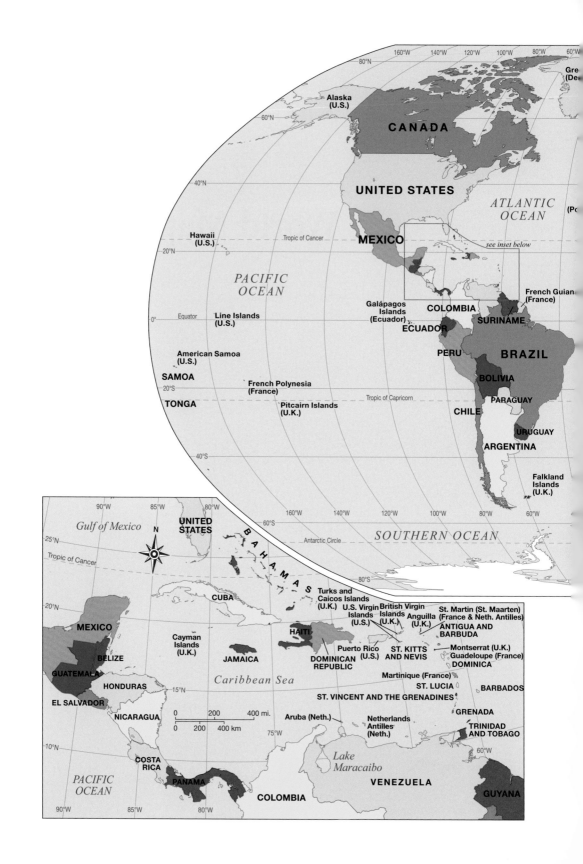

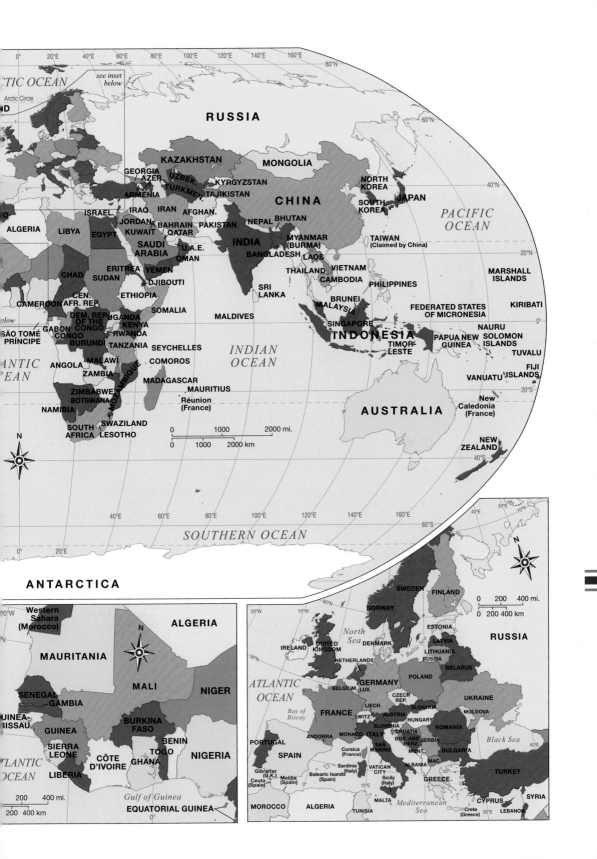

CHAPTER 1

Historical Background on the Oklahoma City Bombing

The Bombing of the Alfred P. Murrah Federal Building, April 19, 1995

Encyclopedia of Terrorism

The following essay provides an objective overview of the Oklahoma City bombing. On April 19, 1995, a two-ton bomb located in a rented truck exploded in Oklahoma City, destroying most of the Alfred P. Murrah Federal Building and killing 168 people, including 19 children and 8 federal workers. Timothy McVeigh was quickly identified as the bomber and Terry Lynn Nichols as one of McVeigh's collaborators. In separate trials, both men were found guilty, despite defense attempts to introduce several conspiracy theories into the proceedings. McVeigh was found guilty and executed on June 11, 2001. Nichols received a life sentence. On April 19, 2000, the Oklahoma City National Memorial and Museum was dedicated to the victims of the attack.

Photo on previous page: The Alfred P. Murrah Federal Building in downtown Oklahoma City was the target of a domestic terrorist's bomb-laden van on Wednesday, April 19, 1995. The explosion killed 168 people. (**Associated Press**.)

The 1995 bombing of the Alfred P. Murrah Federal Building in Oklahoma City, Oklahoma, is among the worst acts of domestic terrorism committed on U.S. soil. Although the two main suspects in the bombing, Timothy McVeigh and Terry Lynn Nichols, were both tried and found guilty, questions about a larger conspiracy remain.

> The bomb destroyed over one-third of the nine-story building, including a day care center located on the second floor. In all, 168 people, including 19 children . . . perished.

On April 19, 1995, at 9:02 A.M., a rented Ryder truck carrying a 4,000-pound fertilizer bomb exploded in front of the Murrah building in Oklahoma City. The bomb destroyed over one-third of the nine-story building, including a day care center located on the second floor. In all, 168 people, including 19 children and eight federal employees, perished; more than 500 were injured.

Two days later, Timothy James McVeigh, then 26, was charged in connection with the bombing. Amid throngs of spectators yelling "baby killer!" and "murderer!" authorities led McVeigh out of the Noble County Jail in Perry, Oklahoma, where he had been held on misdemeanor charges unrelated to the bombing. That same day, Terry Lynn Nichols, then 39, turned himself in to the police in Herington, Kansas, where he was held as a material witness before being formally charged in connection with the bombing. A third possible suspect, identified only as John Doe No. 2 from a police sketch, remained at large.

Rescue workers and investigators continued to comb the rubble for nearly a month. On May 23, 1995, 150 pounds of dynamite were used to implode what remained of the Murrah building. By then, preliminary hearings had already begun. In late August 1995, a federal grand jury indicted McVeigh and Nichols on murder and conspiracy charges. Two years would pass before either would go to trial.

The Trial of Timothy McVeigh

Opening statements for *United States v. McVeigh* began on April 24, 1997, in a Denver, Colorado, courtroom. The government presented several points: McVeigh's antigovernment beliefs; his anger over the government-initiated sieges in Waco, Texas, and Ruby Ridge, Idaho; forensic evidence; telephone and rental records; John Doe No. 1 sightings; the facts of McVeigh's initial traffic arrest on Interstate 35; and key testimony from McVeigh's Army buddy Michael Fortier, his wife, Lori, and McVeigh's sister, Jennifer. Jennifer McVeigh testified to Timothy's ascent from antigovernment protest to "direct action," while Michael and Lori Fortier, who traded their testimony for lesser charges and immunity, respectively, told the court of McVeigh's plan, hatched, the government asserted, in September 1994, as well as their roles in aiding his efforts. The judge also allowed highly emotional testimony from survivors and victims' family members, which often brought the jury of seven men and five women to tears.

> [Timothy] McVeigh's defense team . . . launched a large and expensive independent investigation focusing on the possibility that the conspiracy included many more individuals.

McVeigh's defense team, in the months preceding the trial, launched a large and expensive independent investigation focusing on the possibility that the conspiracy included many more individuals, not just McVeigh and Nichols. Stephen Jones, McVeigh's chief defense counsel, made an early assertion that the two men, if guilty, did not have the resources to carry off the bombing on their own. The defense suggested possible links with Islamic militants based in the Philippines, neo-Nazis, Iraq, and Elohim City, the nearby Christian Identity compound. Jones also claimed that the government, through its various agencies, was suppressing evidence that proved it knew of the planned attack beforehand and could have prevented it. These claims, which were suppressed in court but made known through public records and in Jones's book, *Others Unknown* (1998), have been the basis for the persistent conspiracy theories surrounding the Oklahoma City bombing.

The most alarming connections alleged by the defense's investigation, especially in light of the September 11, 2001, terrorist attacks on the United States involved Nichols's repeated trips to the Philippines. Nichols first traveled to the Philippines in 1990 to meet his mail-order bride, Marife Torres. Nichols returned several times, ostensibly researching "business opportunities." Before his final trip, in November 1994, Nichols gave his former wife, Lana Padilla, a package to be opened in the event of his death. Padilla opened the package soon after Nichols departed, finding therein a significant amount of cash, stolen valuables, wigs, a life insurance policy, and a letter from Nichols to McVeigh. That letter urged McVeigh, "Go for it!"

The Defense Offers Conspiracy Theories

Further investigation into Nichols's Philippine trips revealed a meeting, in the early 1990s, between an American, known only as "the Farmer," and several now-imprisoned terrorists—including Ramzi Ahmed Yousef, Wali Khan Amin Shah, and Abdul Hakim Murad—in wich bomb making and other terrorist activities were discussed. An incarcerated informant and former member of the terrorist group Abu Savyaf identified "the Farmer" as Terry Nichols. Jones's investigation also placed Osama bin Laden in the Philippines in the early 1990s—Nichols was in the Philippines at that time. One of Jones's hypotheses was that McVeigh and Nichols took the fall for a larger conspiracy, much as the Arab men who rented the Ryder truck used in the 1993 World Trade Center bombing were convicted while Ramzi Yousef escaped.

A wall at the Oklahoma City National Memorial Center shows photos of the victims of the bombing. (AP Photo/ Laura Rauch.)

The defense also made significant links between McVeigh and neo-Nazi elements in the United States, most of whom were connected to Elohim City, a white supremacist compound near the Oklahoma-Arkansas border. In the early 1980s, members of the Covenant, the Sword, and the Arm of the Lord (CSA), including a man named Richard Wayne Snell, plotted to blow up the Murrah building in retaliation for the death of Gordon Kahl. (Kahl was a member of the white supremacist group Posse Comitatus who was killed by federal agents.) This plot, however, was never implemented. Snell was later sentenced to death and executed for two separate, unrelated murders. His execution fell on April 19, 1995, the day of the Oklahoma City bombing, as well as the second anniversary of the raid on Waco, Patriot's Day,

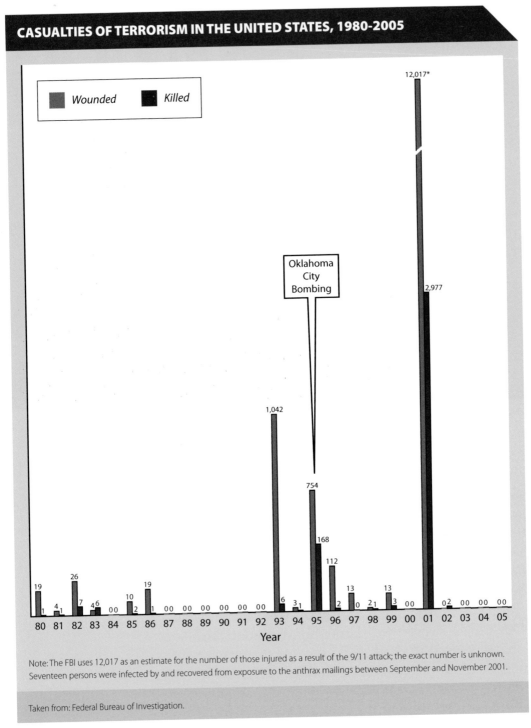

CASUALTIES OF TERRORISM IN THE UNITED STATES, 1980-2005

Wounded ■ Killed

12,017*

Oklahoma
City
Bombing

2,977

1,042

754

168

112

19
26
19
10
13
13
2
02

1
4 1
7 46
00
2
1
00 00 00 00 00 00
6
3 1
2
0
2 1
3
00
00 00 00

80 81 82 83 84 85 86 87 88 89 90 91 92 93 94 95 96 97 98 99 00 01 02 03 04 05

Year

Note: The FBI uses 12,017 as an estimate for the number of those injured as a result of the 9/11 attack; the exact number is unknown. Seventeen persons were infected by and recovered from exposure to the anthrax mailings between September and November 2001.

Taken from: Federal Bureau of Investigation.

and the anniversary of the Battle of Lexington and Concord, where citizen militia groups attacked the English government in 1775.

The defense also made much of McVeigh's phone call to Andreas Carl Strassmeir, a German neo-Nazi living in Elohim City. Although McVeigh maintained, after his conviction, that he had met Strassmeir at a gun show and was calling to inquire about places to hide after the bombing, the defense claimed that the connections were much deeper. Strassmeir had roomed with a man named Michael Brescia, a member of the Aryan Republican Army, and was strongly suspected by the authorities of being John Doe No. 2. Strassmeir was also allegedly connected to Dennis Mahon, a Klansman who ran paramilitary training at Elohim City. Mahon was fervently antigovernment, had allegedly received money from the Iraqi government for several years following the Gulf War, and was identified by Interpol as an international terrorist.

Elohim City also produced a possible defense witness named Carol Howe, a paid informant for the Bureau of Alcohol, Tobacco and Firearms (ATF) who knew both Mahon and Strassmeir. Howe provided the ATF information suggesting that both men had contemplated and/or threatened direct action against the government, including blowing up federal buildings in Oklahoma City and Tulsa. The prosecution, led by Beth Wilkinson, repeatedly asserted that neither Strassmeir nor Mahon was considered to be a suspect. Jones hoped to reveal FBI and/or government negligence for not pursuing these leads.

The Judge Rules Conspiracy Evidence Inadmissable

Judge Richard P. Matsch eventually ruled that the evidence relating to Mahon, Strassmeir, Elohim City, and Howe was "not sufficiently relevant to be admissible," thus eliminating the basis of Jones's wider conspiracy argument. (Jones had abandoned the Philippines-based conspiracy argument when his main informant changed details of his story.) The defense team then focused on discrediting the Fortiers' testimony and revealing the holes in the FBI investigation, including an unidentified and unaccounted-for severed leg found in the rubble, which Jones asserted was that of the "real" bomber, as well as suggestions that the FBI's forensic methods were insufficiently rigorous.

> McVeigh was sentenced to death by lethal injection.

On June 13, 1997, McVeigh was sentenced to death by lethal injection. After McVeigh's well-publicized complaints about Jones's competency, in August, Jones stepped down as the lawyer for the appeals process. McVeigh would eventually decline to move forward with his appeals, and he was sent to a prison in Terre Haute, Indiana, to await execution.

The Trial of Terry Nichols

Terry Lynn Nichols went on trial in November 1997. Nichols faced the same charges as McVeigh, and much of the same evidence and testimony was used in his trial. However, because Nichols was at home in Kansas when the bombing occurred, and because he lacked the motive that the prosecution had established for McVeigh, Nichols was found guilty on only one charge of conspiracy and on eight charges of involuntary manslaughter. In April 1998, Nichols rejected an offer of leniency in exchange for more information about the bombing because he could still be prosecuted by the state of Oklahoma for murder.

A Grand Jury Rejects All Conspiracy Theories

On December 31, 1998, after a year and a half of investigation, a grand jury discounted all theories presented by McVeigh's original defense team, including the existence of John Doe No. 2, wider foreign involvement, and speculation that the federal government had prior warning about the bombing and chose not to act. Following McVeigh's execution on June 11, 2001, the only hope for more answers about the Oklahoma City bombing lies in a possible state trial of Terry Lynn Nichols.

Today, a reflecting pool surrounded by 168 chairs, 149 for each of the adult victims and 19 smaller chairs for the children, is the memorial to those killed in the Oklahoma City bombing. The Survivor Tree, an American elm that somehow withstood the explosion, overlooks the scene.

Two Suspects Are Arrested in Connection with the Oklahoma City Bombing

Michael Whiteley and Susan Roth

In the following viewpoint a Little Rock, Arkansas, newspaper reports on the immediate aftermath of the Oklahoma City bombing, including the arrest of Timothy McVeigh. McVeigh was picked up on a minor traffic charge a couple of days after the bombing; while he was being held, however, he was identified as a prime suspect in the attack. Terry Nichols, a second suspect, turned himself in to the police three days after the blast, according to the authors. The writers also report that several Middle Eastern men who had been held for questioning were released. At the scene of the bombing, rescue workers continued to search for survivors, but increasingly, the effort turned more toward the recovery and *identification of bodies. Michael Whiteley and Susan Roth were staff writers at the Arkansas Democrat-Gazette when this viewpoint was written.*

Two suspects linked to an anti-government extremist group were being held Friday [April 21, 1995] in connection with the bombing of the Alfred P. Murrah Federal Building here.

Federal investigators learned Friday that one of men, identified as Timothy McVeigh, 26, was being held in nearby Perry, Okla., after being stopped on a traffic charge Wednesday about two hours after the bombing.

A second suspect, identified as Terry Nichols, 33, surrendered to authorities Friday afternoon in Herington, Kan., about 35 miles south of Junction City, Kan., where investigators said McVeigh rented a truck later crammed with explosives that were detonated outside the building.

> A former co-worker told [FBI] agents McVeigh had extreme right-wing views.

The FBI said a former co-worker told agents McVeigh had extreme right-wing views and was deeply agitated by the fiery federal attack on the Branch Davidian compound near Waco, Texas, exactly two years before the Oklahoma City bombing.

McVeigh had been so agitated "that he had personally visited the site. After visiting the site, McVeigh expressed extreme anger at the federal government and advised that the government never should have done what it did," according to court documents.

Friday night, authorities put the confirmed deaths in the blast at 78. But they feared that the number killed would climb well into three figures in the next few days as workers sift through the debris of [the] shattered nine-story structure.

McVeigh's Arrest

McVeigh, driving a beat-up yellow Mercury Grand Marquis, was stopped Wednesday for speeding. Police arrested him for possessing a weapon and held him until Friday in Perry, a town of 5,000 people about an hour's drive north of Oklahoma City.

> Police said McVeigh rented the truck under a bogus name and birth date, giving . . . a date significant to members of the Michigan Citizen Militia extremist group.

McVeigh, whose appearance approximates that of a composite sketch released Thursday and identified then as "John Doe No. 1," reportedly is a munitions expert and a native of Pendleton, N.Y., near Niagara Falls. He allegedly rented the truck used in the bombing from a Ryder rental agency in Junction City, about 15 miles from Fort Riley.

Local media reported that Sarah Kennedy, a Perry lawyer, had received a collect call from McVeigh at 9:15 A.M. Friday. Kennedy said he asked for legal representation, telling her he had been arrested on charges of having no driver's license and a weapon violation.

Kennedy said she refused to take the call and, when she learned he was a suspect in the bombing, said she would never consider representing him.

Police said McVeigh rented the truck under a bogus name and birth date, giving his name as Robert Kling and his birthday as April 19, the day of the bombing and a date significant to members of the Michigan Citizen Militia extremist group.

April 19, besides being the date the Branch Davidian compound burned in Waco in 1993, corresponds with the Battle of Concord, which took place on April 19, 1775, and was the opening battle of the Revolutionary War and resulted in a defeat for the British.

Friday afternoon, as a crowd of 500 onlookers jeered, a cluster of federal agents escorted McVeigh from the Noble County Courthouse.

Friday evening, he was flown by helicopter to Tinker Air Force Base outside Oklahoma City for an appearance before federal Magistrate Ronald L. Howland. He was charged there with federal counts of malicious endangerment and destroying a federal building with explosives. The government is seeking the death penalty.

About 10 P.M., McVeigh was transferred to the federal prison at El Reno, near Oklahoma City.

An arrest warrant issued earlier Friday accused him of "malicious danger and destroying by means of an explosive a building or real property, whole or in part, possessed or used in the United States of America."

FBI agents escort Timothy McVeigh out of the Noble County, Oklahoma, courthouse on April 21, 1995, after he was charged for his involvement in the Oklahoma City bombing. (**Bob Daemmerich/ AFP/Getty Images.**)

Using Forensic Science to Identify Victims

Although forensic science played a role in the investigation of the [Oklahoma City] bombing, its chief role was in victim identification. Some of the bodies were complete enough to allow for fingerprint identification, but many were fragmented, making the work of identification painstaking and arduous. The forensic investigators' first step was to gather antemortem [before death] information, including lists of people who were believed to be at or near the bombsite. Families and funeral directors provided demographic information, and potential victims' dentists were contacted to provide records. A prominent role was played by forensic odontologists, who faced the grim task of identifying the remains of the victims from teeth. They estimated the age of children based on patterns of primary and permanent teeth. Many of these children had pieces of wallboard embedded in their teeth, suggesting that the explosion had blown them through the wall of the day care center.

After a body was discovered, an average of fifteen x-rays of it were taken. Pathologists, anthropologists, and FBI bomb specialists examined these x-rays to identify the victims as well as to uncover crime scene evidence. In many cases, the x-rays revealed either healed fractures or degenerative conditions. One victim, for example, was identified from degenerative changes in the spine; another was identified from healed fractures in the tibia and fibula. X-rays of missing persons who were thought to be victims of the bombing were compared with these postmortem x-rays for

Terry Nichols Is Associated with the Michigan Militia

The second suspect, who U.S. Attorney General Janet Reno said resembles a man sought as "John Doe No. 2," is the brother of James Douglas Nichols, who owns a house authorities raided in Decker, Mich. McVeigh's driver's license reportedly lists the Decker address as his own.

Investigators believe James Douglas Nichols is associated with the anti-government movement in Michigan. Terry Nichols attended a meeting of the Michigan Citizen Militia. The group was reportedly formed in April 1994 in opposition to federal gun control laws.

possible matches. X-rays also revealed the presence of foreign objects in the bodies, including evidence of the bomb itself, and they were used to distinguish bomb evidence from leaded-glass shards from the building's windows.

Finally, forensic anthropologists also played a key role in victim identification. In many instances, only a single disembodied body part was found, and body parts were often commingled. Forensic anthropologists could, for example, measure a limb, then use a computer program that determines age and race from bone measurements to pin down the demographics of the victim, which could then be compared with antemortem information to provide a possible match. . . .

By the time all of the victims had been identified three weeks after the explosion, forty-four had been identified through teeth alone; twenty-five through fingerprints alone; seventy-seven through a combination of teeth and fingerprints; one through teeth and palm prints; one through teeth, fingerprints, and DNA; six through x-rays alone; four through palm prints; three through DNA alone; one through footprints; one through a toe print; one through marks and scars; and four through visual identification.

SOURCE. *K. Lee Lerner and Brenda Wilmoth Lerner, eds.,* World of Forensic Science, *vol. 2. Detroit: Gale, 2005. pp. 495–498.*

Early Friday, the Justice Department announced that the FBI had released a Palestinian-American detained in London and returned to the United States on Thursday. The man had left Oklahoma City shortly after the bombing, and flew from Chicago to London. And in Dallas, brothers Anis Siddiqy, 24, and Asad R. Siddiqy, 27, and a third man, Mohammed Chafi, were all released after being questioned about the case Wednesday.

Meanwhile, officials at the blast site expanded the nine-block area cordoned off earlier, moving the perimeters two or three more blocks to the south and west sides of the building. Oklahoma City fire officials said they needed to search the larger area for debris and evidence from the explosion. The bomb exploded on the north side of building.

About 12:45 P.M. Friday, weary but determined workers placed an American flag on a crane at the northwest corner of the smashed building. President [Bill] Clinton had ordered flags across the country lowered to half-staff Thursday in honor of the dead.

Clinton planned to travel here this weekend and was scheduled to lead special memorial services Sunday with the Rev. Billy Graham.

The Rescue, Recovery, and Identification of Victims

Good weather so far has aided rescue crews, but officials expected rain Saturday, with a high temperature of about 57 and wind chill in [the] low 40s. Fire officials said a wind picking up from the north could blow rain into building, complicating or halting rescue efforts because of the weakened condition of the structure.

> Officials were using dental records, fingerprints and, in some cases, footprints to identify the dead.

Ray Blakeney, Oklahoma medical examiner, said officials were using dental records, fingerprints and, in some cases, footprints to identify the dead.

"We are also going to homes and talking to people," he said.

Earlier in the day, authorities said they were beginning to find pockets filled with corpses as workers moved material out of the way. Crews confined their search Friday to the first three floors of the building, the basement and garage.

"We'll hold out hope to find survivors until the day we move off the building, but we've pulled off floors three and above," Fire Chief Gary Marrs said.

The lower floors are believed to contain all the remaining bodies under layers of rubble from each of the floors that fell, creating a pancake effect and extremely difficult work for the crews.

James Lee Witt, the director of the Federal Emergency Management Agency [FEMA], said he had requested a public health service team to help the state medical examiner's office identify bodies. The agency brought in equipment as well, including portable X-ray machines.

> FBI agents . . . questioned business owners and residents to piece together the whereabouts of McVeigh and Terry Nichols in the days before the bombing.

But Witt said FEMA workers couldn't get into the devastated building yet because it's still considered a crime scene.

"That makes it different from a natural disaster," Witt said. "We will do a preliminary assessment of the building as soon as the building is released as a crime scene."

Witt also estimated that about 75 buildings downtown sustained some damage in the blast, though he couldn't say yet whether that damage was structural or minor in all cases.

But fire officials said other buildings near the bomb site look just as bad as the Murrah building, though they may not be as large. Others may have died in these buildings or in cars that were crushed like tin cans in the explosion.

Witnesses Are Questioned

FBI agents Thursday and Friday questioned business owners and residents to piece together the whereabouts of McVeigh and Terry Nichols in the days before the bombing.

Sylvia Niemczyk, manager of the Texaco Food Mart in Junction City, said the two men often entered the business to buy gas, snack food, cokes and other items sold at the convenience store.

"They kind of kept to themselves," Niemczyk recalled Friday. The two spoke little and always paid in cash, she said.

"Nobody really knew them personally. They were nice customers, really. Clean-cut. They weren't mean or rude. They just came in, did their business and left."

Niemczyk said she didn't know their names and never noticed what kind of vehicle they drove.

Dave Russell, an official with Ryder Truck Rental in Junction City, said FBI officials questioned him in connection with the Oklahoma bombing, but he wouldn't comment further.

Ronald Moore told The Associated Press he recalled seeing a man resembling one of the suspects pictured in composite sketches released by the FBI at a Junction City convenience store on Monday or Tuesday. He said the man was standing on the passenger side of a yellow rental truck.

Moore said the man was pumping gas into a 5-gallon plastic jug that was sitting on the floor in the passenger side of the truck. Moore chided the man for putting gas into a plastic container.

"I looked at him and said, 'That might dissolve,'" Moore recalled. "I called him stupid."

"I thought they were just GIs" from nearby Fort Riley, Moore said. "I see a lot of them around here."

Gasoline could have been one of the ingredients needed to make the bomb, an explosives expert said.

Daniel Fetterly of the United Service Associates, a Los Angeles-based global team of law enforcement and military experts, said a fertilizer-and-diesel-fuel bomb like that used in the Oklahoma City blast probably would use gasoline as detonator.

The President Offers Sympathy and Support to the Victims

Bill Clinton

In the following speech, the US president speaks to families and survivors of the Oklahoma City bombing at a memorial service on April 23, 1995, just four days after the tragedy. He thanks rescue workers for their heroic service and promises survivors that the United States will do everything possible to help heal the city's wounds and bring to justice the person or persons guilty of the crime. He urges listeners not to give in to hatred, but to stand up against fear and violence, and to dedicate their lives to overcoming evil with good. Bill Clinton was the 42nd president of the United States, serving from 1993 to 2001.

SOURCE. William J. Clinton, "Remarks at a Memorial Service for the Bombing Victims in Oklahoma City, Oklahoma: April 23, 1995," Administration of William J. Clinton, Public Papers of the President of the United States, Books I and II, 1995, pp. 573–574.

Thank you very much. [Oklahoma] Governor [Frank A.] Keating and Mrs. [Cathy] Keating, Reverend [Billy] Graham, to the families of those who have been lost and wounded, to the people of Oklahoma City who have endured so much, and the people of this wonderful State, to all of you who are here as our fellow Americans: I am honored to be here today to represent the American people. But I have to tell you that Hillary and I also come as parents, as husband and wife, as people who were your neighbors for some of the best years of our lives.

A Nation Joins in Grief

Today our Nation joins with you in grief. We mourn with you. We share your hope against hope that some may still survive. We thank all those who have worked so heroically to save lives and to solve this crime, those here in Oklahoma and those who are all across this great land and many who left their own lives to come here to work hand in hand with you.

> We pledge to do all we can to help you heal the injured, to rebuild this city, and to bring to justice those who did this evil.

We pledge to do all we can to help you heal the injured, to rebuild this city, and to bring to justice those who did this evil.

This terrible sin took the lives of our American family: innocent children, in that building only because their parents were trying to be good parents as well as good workers; citizens in the building going about their daily business; and many there who served the rest of us, who worked to help the elderly and the disabled, who worked to support our farmers and our veterans, who worked to enforce our laws and to protect us. Let us say clearly, they served us well, and we are grateful. But for so many of you they were also neighbors and friends. You saw them at church or the PTA meetings, at the civic clubs,

at the ball park. You know them in ways that all the rest of America could not.

And to all the members of the families here present who have suffered loss, though we share your grief, your pain is unimaginable, and we know that. We cannot undo it. That is God's work.

Our words seem small beside the loss you have endured. But I found a few I wanted to share today. I've received a lot of letters in these last terrible days. One stood out because it came from a young widow and a mother of three whose own husband was murdered with over

President and Mrs. Clinton attend a memorial service for the victims of the Oklahoma bombing four days after the tragedy. The men next to the President hold teddy bears given to children of affected families. (AP Photo/Beth A. Keiser.)

200 other Americans when Pan Am 103 was shot down.[1] Here is what that woman said I should say to you today: "The anger you feel is valid, but you must not allow yourselves to be consumed by it. The hurt you feel must not be allowed to turn into hate but instead into the search for justice. The loss you feel must not paralyze your own lives. Instead, you must try to pay tribute to your loved ones by continuing to do all the things they left undone, thus ensuring they did not die in vain." Wise words from one who also knows.

You have lost too much, but you have not lost everything. And you have certainly not lost America, for we will stand with you for as many tomorrows as it takes.

If ever we needed evidence of that, I could only recall the words of Governor and Mrs. Keating. If anybody thinks that Americans are mostly mean and selfish, they ought to come to Oklahoma. If anybody thinks Americans have lost the capacity for love and caring and courage, they ought to come to Oklahoma.

To all my fellow Americans beyond this hall, I say, one thing we owe those who have sacrificed is the duty to purge ourselves of the dark forces which gave rise to this evil. They are forces that threaten our common peace, our freedom, our way of life.

Lessons to Impart to Our Children

Let us teach our children that the God of comfort is also the God of righteousness. Those who trouble their own house will inherit the wind. Justice will prevail.

Let us let our own children know that we will stand against the forces of fear. When there is talk of hatred, let us stand up and talk against it. When there is talk of violence, let us stand up and talk against it. In the face of death, let us honor life. As St. Paul admonished us, let us not be overcome by evil but overcome evil with good.

Yesterday Hillary and I had the privilege of speaking with some children of other Federal employees, children like those who were lost here. And one little girl said something we will never forget. She said we should all plant a tree in memory of the children. So this morning before we got on the plane to come here, at the White House, we planted that tree in honor of the children of Oklahoma. It was a dogwood with its wonderful

> Those who are lost now belong to God. Some day we will be with them. But until that happens, their legacy must be our lives.

spring flower and its deep, enduring roots. It embodies the lesson of the Psalms that the life of a good person is like a tree whose leaf does not wither.

My fellow Americans, a tree takes a long time to grow, and wounds take a long time to heal. But we must begin. Those who are lost now belong to God. Some day we will be with them. But until that happens, their legacy must be our lives.

Thank you all, and God bless you.

Note

1. On December 21, 1988, a terrorist bomb downed Pan Am flight 103 over Lockerbie, Scotland. Libyan ruler Muammar Gaddafi claimed responsibility.

Domestic Terrorists Are to Blame for the Bombing

Ed Vulliamy

In the following essay, a British journalist reports on the arrest of Timothy McVeigh and the detainment of Terry and James Nichols in connection with the Oklahoma City bombing. Initially, investigators thought the perpetrators were Islamic terrorists or members of a drug cartel; eventually their investigation led them to McVeigh and the Nicholses, members of an extremist militia movement that views the federal government as its greatest enemy. The author reviews the military background of the men and links the timing of the bombing to the Battle of Concord during the American Revolution in 1775, and the showdown between Branch Davidian religious sect leader David Koresh and federal law enforcement officers at Waco, Texas, in 1993. At the time this viewpoint was written, Ed Vulliamy was the New York correspondent for the London *Observer*.

SOURCE. Ed Vulliamy, "The Enemy Within," *The Observer*, April 23, 1995, p. 14. Copyright © Guardian News & Media Ltd., 1995. All rights reserved. Reproduced by permission.

With the death toll from the Oklahoma City blast standing at 81 and another 150 people unaccounted for yesterday, America had to face the prospect that it had witnessed the first ghastly shot in a war declared by its burgeoning fascist militia movement.

US army veteran Timothy McVeigh, who is charged with planting the bomb, belongs to a movement that has grown up in recent years, imbued with an irrational hatred of federal government.

Two other men, Terry Nichols, and his brother, James, who are being detained as material witnesses but not suspects, are also members. They can be held until court hearings on Thursday [April 27, 1993].

> "US army veteran Timothy McVeigh . . . belongs to a movement that has grown up in recent years, imbued with an irrational hatred of the federal government."

The Militia Movement and Timothy McVeigh

The movement's adherents train, either openly or in secret, in preparation for confrontation with what they loosely define as the enemy—the federal government. They claim they are acting in defence of the Constitution.

The movement includes among its founders veteran right-wing extremists, one of whom [Bo Gritz, also spelled Greitz] was able last week to describe the horror at the Alfred P. Murrah Federal Building where a children's nursery took the blast's full force, as "a Rembrandt, a masterpiece of science and art put together".

McVeigh, a 27-year-old army veteran of the Operation Desert Storm in the [first] Gulf war, made no secret of his affiliations to the Right and is a member of the Michigan Militia—a branch of the paramilitary network.

An earlier report that he, like so many members of the militia movement, had left a message on the Internet was revealed by the FBI yesterday to be a hoax. The false message purported to identify him as the Mad Bomber and signed off with a "Boom!".

It emerged yesterday that in recent weeks he was among demonstrators outside the prison where white supremacist Richard Snell was executed on the same day as the Oklahoma bomb for the murder of a Jewish businessman and black policeman.

He was also said by colleagues in the militia, and in the indictment against him, to have been a passionate sympathiser of the stand taken by David Koresh's Branch Davidian cult, overcome by government agents at Waco, Texas [in 1993]. The carnage in Oklahoma occurred on the second anniversary of the Waco siege.

The investigation has turned full circle since the 4,000 lb car bomb decimated the government office block in the city centre at 9.30 A.M. last Wednesday.

The authorities were initially struck by the coincidence of the date.

The investigation into the Branch Davidian cult and the final storming of its armed sanctuary had been led by the FBI's Robert Ricks, based at the Oklahoma building, and now the team suspected a reprisal.

They didn't realise how close they were to the truth, for they eventually discarded that trail in favour of another: extremist Islam. The bomb resembled that which razed the American embassy in Beirut; Oklahoma had connections with fundamentalist Islamic groups, and was once the venue for a convention of Afghan militants.

A Jordanian-American was picked up at London's Heathrow airport and flown back for questioning.

This trail fell in favour of another theory early on Friday: narcotics-trafficking cartels striking back at the offices of the Drug Enforcement Administration. Then this in turn came

> It was revealed that the enemy came not from the Mid-East, but possibly from the Midwest, not from without but from within.

to nothing, as it was revealed that the enemy came not from the Mid-East, but possibly from the Midwest, not from without but from within. A sudden and brilliant flurry of activity by the law-enforcement agencies unveiled the alleged origin of the monstrous attack. America may be an easy place to carry out a terrorist attack, but it is a very difficult place in which to avoid detection.

The axle of the explosive-laden truck was found, and linked to a video taken of a Ryder rental van parked outside the office block. The van, it was discovered, had been leased at Junction City, in neighbouring Kansas, from Elliot's Body Shop, whose owner gave the police strikingly accurate descriptions of his two clients. Drawings were published, and warrants issued for their arrest. Extraordinarily, one of the suspects was already in custody—McVeigh, a native of New York. Only an hour after the explosion, he had been caught speeding at 90 mph in a car without a number plate. He was then found to possess a loaded revolver and detained at Perry, a small town due north of Oklahoma City.

Under the law, McVeigh could have been released on bail on Friday morning, but on seeing the identikit pictures, the Perry traffic police went back to take another look at him and at his driving licence.

McVeigh's Michigan Connection

The address on the licence was that of a farm in Michigan, belonging to James Nichols. Within minutes, squads of armed FBI agents had surrounded the house at Decker, Michigan, whose owner turned out to be a member of the local Michigan Milita. The militia was one of the network of "survivalist" and armed anti-government groups, well known to the authorities and even the subject of a lengthy television documentary.

Nichols was described by his neighbours as "a sovereign citizen"—a man who had refused to pay his car tax, and who "resented paying property tax and income tax".

People walk on the Berlin Wall in front of the Brandenburg Gate in November of 1989. The militia movement followers believed the fall of the wall heralded the dawn of a "New World Order." (**AP Photo.**)

Later, it emerged that he was also a small-time arms dealer and a specialist in explosives. He was taken in after a stand-off lasting some hours, but was said to be "co-operating". Yesterday he was moved and held in Detroit.

Meanwhile, another name had been published, that of Terry Nichols, brother to James and connected to the Michigan Militia. He also served in the US Infantry alongside McVeigh and lived in Herington, Kansas.

A second driving licence, discovered yesterday, (US drivers need new licences when they move state) and dated November 1993, shows McVeigh's address at that time as the US Army's barracks at Fort Riley, near Junction City in Kansas, thus linking him to the Prairie state.

Terry Nichols was a dealer in military surplus equipment. The owner of a cable television firm in the area said that he had been to Nichols's home last Friday morning to install extra channels on his set. He had "wanted to watch the coverage of the bomb".

Terry gave himself up to the authorities during the afternoon. He was said to be "co-operating", and was being held in Abilene.

Late on Friday afternoon, McVeigh emerged from the Perry police station to shouts of "Baby Killer!" from a hostile crowd. He was dressed in an orange prison tunic, his face hard-set, his hair cropped. He was taken by helicopter to the Tinker Air Force base near Oklahoma City, and then to the El Reno federal jail, and charged with "malicious endangerment and destruction by means of explosives of a federal building".

His deportment was described by one official as "very militaristic—'yes sir, no sir'. He said nothing in contradiction or admission of the charges." Yesterday he was moved to Oklahoma County Jail.

McVeigh and Terry Nichols have both served in the military—the former is said to be a munitions expert. An army yearbook of soldiers at the Fort Benning barracks in Georgia has a picture of McVeigh and a man believed to be Terry Nichols making a bomb, as well as their mugshots.

The Michigan Militia had been markedly vocal in its support for Koresh's Branch Davidian cult. The "Bill of Information", under which McVeigh was charged, quotes a colleague interviewed by the FBI as saying that McVeigh was "particularly agitated by the raid on Waco Texas . . . so agitated that he had personally visited the site."

The citation talks of his "extreme right-wing views" and "extreme anger at the federal government over Waco". The authorities said early yesterday that their investigations are "only just beginning", and that the net will widen; three more men are sought immediately, two believed to be in Oklahoma City. President [Bill] Clinton promised his Justice Department will find the bombers, "convict them, and we will seek the death penalty."

The militias, organised in 40 of the 50 states, sit within an ideological movemement which has gained ground steadily in America during the past two years. For some time, small armed groups called "Survivalists" have organised in remote areas motivated by a form of "outward bound", right-wing politics and preparing for the aftermath of nuclear war.

For the Militia, the Enemy Is Washington

But after the demise of the Soviet threat, a new, armed right-wing movement started to replace them. To these new groups, the enemy was not in Moscow, but in Washington. One supporter claimed at a recent convention of mercenary soldiers in Las Vegas: "Anyone who talks about Communism doesn't get it any more. The enemy is fascism in the White House." Their ideology can be roughly summarised as the extreme version of a general tide of loosely-defined "anti-government" feeling within American politics. Until Friday night, it was regarded as crazed fantasy; now it is the doctrine of mass slaughter.

> [The militias] see the enemy of all Americans, regardless of creed or colour, to be the federal government.

They believe the fall of the Berlin Wall [in 1989] heralded the dawn of a New World Order, dominated by secret powers intent on establishing a global dictatorship. The Clinton administration is regarded by all these groups as a puppet of global forces. Some of the new literature has a militant Christian gist, and describes these powers as "Luciferian" or "Luciferian Globalist". A cult trilogy about a fantastical masonic group called the "Illuminati" is taken seriously, and there is a belief that this occult elite is preparing to coincide a push for world domination with the advent of the third millennium. Such beliefs give the movement an apocalyptic dimension.

A Homegrown Terrorist

At first, most people assumed that the [Oklahoma City] attack was the work of Muslim extremists, but in fact the truth lay a good deal closer to home.

Within two days, the police had arrested a young American named Timothy McVeigh and charged him with the crime. The arrest was a surprise to many who had known McVeigh. A former soldier who had served with distinction during the Persian Gulf War, McVeigh was regarded as a patriotic American who cared deeply for his country. He had grown up in a middle-class family, he had done well in school, and he had never been in trouble with the law. In all these ways, McVeigh seemed an unlikely candidate to be a terrorist.

McVeigh was nevertheless guilty. His act of terror was sparked by an extreme antigovernment perspective. Beginning in his high school days, McVeigh had been drawn to a deeply conservative, or right-wing, political philosophy, the centerpiece of which was a distrust of the federal government. As McVeigh grew older, the distrust turned into a conviction that the U.S. government was a great evil. In his view, the government was infringing on Americans' rights and needed to be stopped. At Oklahoma City that April morning [in 1995], Timothy McVeigh put his ideas into practice.

SOURCE. Stephen Currie, ed., Terrorists and Terrorist Groups, *Lucent Terrorism Library. San Diego: Lucent Books, 2002, pp. 57–68.*

The literature varies considerably on the matter of race, and there is a political penumbra connecting the militias with the neo-Nazi movement, while some pamphlets refer to "cabalistic finance"—a thinly-veiled reference to Jews. But they see the enemy of all Americans, regardless of creed or colour, to be the federal government.

Total immersion in the culture of firearms, military surplus equipment, surveillance equipment and urban warfare gadgetry is a common denominator among all these groups. The favourite magazines are the mercenaries' *Soldier of Fortune* and a mail-order catalogue called *US Cavalry*, peddling paramilitary paraphernalia. McVeigh was a keen subscriber to both.

It is the essence of the American Constitution, says this movement, that a citizen has the right to bear arms, and to form militias. They hark back to the days of the American Revolution as their declared inspiration.

So no arm of the US federal state typifies the perceived assault on what these people call liberty than that charged with enforcing the gun laws: the Bureau of Alcohol, Tobacco and Firearms, the ATF. And this is where Waco comes into frame. Although David Koresh was a deranged maniac, he is seen by the militia movement as a hero, who entrenched his right to arm his citizen followers, who were "murdered" by the ATF.

There is a radio station in Los Angeles called Radio Free World, generally regarded as the broadcast voice of the movement. You can buy tapes of their programmes. They are remarkable documents; one called The Panic Project warns of a mock invasion from outer space being planned by the US government for the year 2000 in order to spread panic and establish an authoritarian government. Another lunatic edition called Nazi '94 likens President Clinton's gun control measures with Hitler's disarming of German citizens prior to the Third Reich.

The fatal 19 April was also the anniversary of another date: the day the British Army fired on the revolutionary militias in Lexington, Massachusetts, in 1775, thereby igniting the American insurrection.

No militia was more eager in its published material to support the stand at Waco than that based in Michigan. Formed in April 1994, they have been happy to prance around in fatigues for television cameras, and for *Time* magazine. Its leader and founder is a former Air Force sergeant, Norman Olsen, a Baptist pastor.

Like most militia leaders on Friday night, Mr Olsen distanced himself from the Oklahoma bombing, but added that its perpetrators "were balancing the scales" after Waco. "They are bringing about what they call a measure for measure, an eye for an eye, a tooth for a tooth."

Dan Stomberg, a friend of McVeigh and the Nichols brothers said: "I've heard James Nichols say that President Clinton should be dead, that he doesn't deserve to live, let alone be President . . . I've watched them make bombs," he added. "Small stuff, nothing like (Oklahoma). You would put two things together that are harmless—fertiliser, chemicals—and it would explode."

And another leading member of the Michigan militia, Phil Marawski, recalled Timothy McVeigh as being "over-zealous". On Waco, "He believed that David Koresh was wrong, but that the government had overstepped the line."

Could these men have committed the massacre at Oklahoma? "I know James (Nichols) wouldn't do that. As for Tim and Terry—well, I've met 100 who have the same ideas and who want to do the same thing. They can talk about it and talk about it, but you don't really believe it will happen until something like this happens. Half the time, you are talking about Waco, half the time, you are at gun shows. Waco was a battle-cry, Waco was a war-cry. These people justify themselves that this is an act of war. They are kind of in a mindset that in a war, all is fair. And if you talk to people of this mindset, you get the feeling that something is going to blow."

But there were still no words to match that of the elderly veteran of the militia and survivalist movement, Bo Greitz. Greitz is leader of an infamous right-wing milita in Idaho. Speaking at a meeting in Dallas on Friday, he came up with the ultimate profanity: "a Rembrandt".

The Trial of Timothy McVeigh: The Prosecution and the Defense Cases

Gordon Witkin

The following essay comprehensively outlines both the prosecution and defense teams' strategies for the imminent trial of Oklahoma City bomber Timothy McVeigh. According to Witkin, the prosecution will demonstrate that first, McVeigh reserved and picked up the rented truck that contained the bomb that blew up the Murrah Federal Building in Oklahoma City; second, he was covered with bomb residue when he was picked up seventy-eight minutes later; and third, he had both "mindset and motive." The defense team will try to demonstrate reasonable doubt by asserting that the FBI crime lab was sloppy in processing evidence; prosecution witnesses are not credible; and that a conspiracy existed leading up to the bombing. At the time of writing this essay, Gordon Witkin

SOURCE. Gordon Witkin, "Making the Case," *U.S. News & World Report*, vol. 122, no. 12, March 31, 1997, pp. 22–24. Copyright © U.S. News & World Report. All rights reserved. Reproduced by permission.

was a senior editor for *U.S. News & World Report*; since 2008, he has been the managing editor for the Center for Public Integrity.

E arly in the trial of Timothy McVeigh, prosecutors will no doubt remind jurors of the carnage created when the Alfred P. Murrah Federal Building in Oklahoma City blew up two years ago. The original indictment included the names of the 168 dead, a list that goes on for more than three full pages. At the bottom of the last page are the names of the children—19 of them aged 5 or under.

The harsh memory may sadden jurors, but in itself won't convict McVeigh. In hopes of doing that, the prosecution has accumulated 25,000 witness statements, 350 audiocassette tapes, 500 videocassette tapes, and more than 30,000 photographs.

> The harsh memory [of the bombing] may sadden jurors, but in itself won't convict McVeigh.

But the trajectory of the trial will be determined as much by a few missing elements. First, the prosecution decided last month that it has no reliable eyewitnesses placing McVeigh in Oklahoma City on the day of the blast. People who claim to have seen him there on that day presented conflicting accounts of who was with him. Second, Judge Richard Matsch ruled last summer that it would be unfair to McVeigh to admit into evidence the nine-hour interview alleged co-conspirator Terry Nichols gave the FBI after the blast, during which he reportedly implicates McVeigh. And Nichols cannot be compelled to testify at this trial since he might, in the process, incriminate himself. Finally, Judge Matsch ruled that McVeigh should be tried separately from Nichols, which makes it more difficult to tie them together in a conspiracy. The net effect is that the prosecution is more vulnerable than it initially appeared.

The first task for the two large teams of attorneys is selecting jurors from a 23-county region of northeast Colorado. That process has become more difficult because of recent stories in the *Dallas Morning News* and on *Playboy* magazine's Internet site alleging that McVeigh has confessed to his defense team. The trial is expected to take two to five months. While each side will have dozens of legal thrusts and counter-thrusts, their basic strategies are already becoming clear.

> The [prosecution's] main task is to put forward a simple syllogism: McVeigh rented a particular Ryder truck. That truck blew up the building. Therefore, McVeigh was behind the bombing.

The prosecution's case. The legal team for the United States government will be led by Joseph Hartzler, 46, a soft-spoken assistant U.S. attorney from Springfield, Ill., who got the job partly on the strength of his successful 1985 prosecution of Puerto Rican nationalists involved in a Chicago bombing plot. Hartzler has multiple sclerosis and will maneuver around the courtroom in a motorized scooter. The team's main task is to put forward a simple syllogism: McVeigh rented a particular Ryder truck. That truck blew up the building. Therefore, McVeigh was behind the bombing. To establish this, they will focus on three key dates and try to prove that:

McVeigh reserved the truck. On the morning of Thursday, April 14, 1995, McVeigh drove a station wagon, smoking from a blown head gasket, into a Junction City, Kan., Firestone tire store, according to the prosecution. Store manager Thomas Manning has said he then sold McVeigh an old Mercury Marquis, in which the suspect was eventually arrested. He also has said that McVeigh left in the middle of the transaction for 15 minutes or so. Prosecutors assert he used that time to make two important phone calls from a bus depot a block away—calls he charged to a prepaid phone calling card that has become crucial to the prosecution's case. The first call went to Nichols's house. The second, at 9:53 A.M., went to Elliott's Body Shop, the agency that rented the Ryder truck. Employees there have told investigators that a man identifying himself as Bob Kling—an alias linked to McVeigh through a phony driver's license—called that morning seeking to rent a truck capable of carrying 5,000 pounds of cargo. Firestone store manager Manning, who has a heart condition, may not actually appear at the trial, but his videotaped testimony could be pivotal.

McVeigh picked up the truck. On Monday, April 17, McVeigh was captured on a videotape at a McDonald's 1 mile from Elliott's Body Shop, according to the prosecution. Twenty to 30 minutes later, at 4:22 P.M., two men— one using the phony Kling driver's license—arrived at Elliott's to pick up the 20-foot Ryder. Shop owner Eldon Elliott and mechanic Tom Kessinger will testify that McVeigh was "Kling." Kessinger has a checkered criminal past, but it was his description that formed the basis of the FBI's original, uncannily accurate composite sketch of McVeigh. At least one other witness will link McVeigh to the truck. Lea McGown, owner of the Dreamland Motel in Junction City, is expected to testify that McVeigh stayed there from April 14 to 18, registered under his own name, and was seen with a Ryder truck.

He was covered with bomb residue. The last key moment, prosecutors believe, came 78 minutes after the bombing, on Interstate 35 near Perry, Okla., some 76 miles north of Oklahoma City. That's where state trooper Charlie Hanger pulled the Mercury Marquis over because it had no license tag and arrested McVeigh for allegedly possessing a weapon. McVeigh's clothes were covered with bomb residue, according to the government's tests. Published reports say a pair of McVeigh's jeans and two shirts he wore that day held traces of PETN, a compound found in detonating cord and blasting caps. In addition, a pair of earplugs found on McVeigh reportedly tested positive for EGDN, which is found in dynamite.

The government will also present a receipt, with McVeigh's fingerprint on it, that recorded the purchase of forty 50-pound bags of ammonium nitrate fertilizer, a key component in the bomb, from the Mid-Kansas Cooperative Association in McPherson, Kan. More important, the FBI found at the bomb site itself ammonium nitrate crystals lodged in a piece of yellow Ryder truck paneling, and an axle whose vehicle identification number told investigators that the truck was rented at Elliott's Body Shop in Junction City.

McVeigh Had Mindset and Motive

He had the mindset and motive. The government is hoping that the basic story chronology will be provided by another former Army pal of McVeigh's, Michael Fortier, who lived near McVeigh in Kingman, Ariz., through much of 1994 and early 1995. Fortier, who initially denied that McVeigh was involved in the bombing, eventually changed his story after pleading guilty in 1995 to helping the defendant transport stolen weapons, and failing to warn the government of the bomb plot. The 27-year-old now faces a sentence of 38 months to 23 years, depending, most likely, on the quality of his testimony.

Fortier reportedly now has a lot to say: that McVeigh was angered by the law enforcement attack on the Branch Davidians at Waco[1] and wanted to "wake up America" to the sins of the federal government; that he and McVeigh "cased" the Murrah building in late 1994; that McVeigh helped organize a 1994 robbery of an Arkansas gun dealer, the proceeds of which allegedly helped fund the bombing; and that McVeigh used soup cans as props to demonstrate how the explosion would destroy the building. Fortier's wife, Lori, who has been given immunity

Assistant US attorney Joseph Hartzler (seated, surrounded by the rest of the prosecution team) talks to the media after Timothy McVeigh was formally sentenced to death. (**AP Photo/Ed Andrieski.**)

from prosecution, is expected to testify that she helped McVeigh create the phony driver's license in the name of Robert Kling of Redfield, S.D. "The Fortiers are the linchpin," says Denver attorney Scott Robinson, who has been writing about the trial. "If the Fortiers are believable, everything falls in place for the prosecution."

The Defense's Case

McVeigh's defense team is led by the theatrical Oklahoma attorney Stephen Jones. A classic faux country lawyer, Jones gives the impression of being a yokel but is a gifted defense attorney. Denver attorney Andrew Cohen, a close trial observer, believes that the government case has several weaknesses for Jones to exploit. "[The government] has to create a chain of evidence based on dribs and drabs here and there," says Cohen. "And circumstantial cases are extra hard to prove when you have good defense lawyers."

To sow reasonable doubt in the minds of jurors, the defense team will try to prove that:

> [Defense attorney Stephen] Jones will contend that widespread contamination at the lab has rendered the positive findings of explosive residue on McVeigh's clothes meaningless.

The FBI crime lab is incompetent. The goal will be to undermine the effectiveness of the forensic evidence through a blistering attack on the FBI crime laboratory—which Jones has called the "potential Detective Mark Fuhrman[2] issue of this case." Jones's star witness will be whistle-blowing FBI chemist Frederic Whitehurst, whose allegations of slipshod procedures and conditions at the lab have led to an internal Justice Department inquiry that is said to support at least some of his charges. With Whitehurst's help, Jones will contend that widespread contamination at the lab has rendered the positive findings of explosive residue on McVeigh's clothes meaningless. The defense will further allege that the lab lacks formal rules for its testing. What it has instead, charges Whitehurst in a deposition, "is a kind of oral tradition, like medieval English . . . and the advantage of the oral tradition is that nobody knows what it is."

The government stoically claims to be unconcerned by the lab problems. For one thing, said assistant prosecutor Beth Wilkinson in a hearing last fall, the idea that explosive residue is floating all over the lab, and thus contaminating the facility, is belied by the fact that there are only six positive reports of high-explosive residue in the case out of 404 tests conducted. Prosecutors are placing great faith in their primary lab witness, FBI chemist Steven Burmeister, whom even Whitehurst calls "brilliant."

To counter the prosecution's heavy reliance on the "Bridges Phone Card," defense attorneys will assert that the records of the call to the body shop lack an ID number and that it can't be traced to McVeigh.

The witnesses were either confused or coerced. Jones will argue that Michael Fortier is falsely implicating McVeigh solely to get his prison sentence reduced, and he will cite hundreds of hours of FBI tapes—prior to the plea bargain—on which the Fortiers profess McVeigh's innocence. Published reports indicate that the defense also may use the Fortiers' admitted drug use to paint them as being memory-impaired.

The tire-store manager, Thomas Manning, will be challenged for what the defense claims is a curious 11th-hour conversion. Although Manning said in his November deposition that McVeigh had left the store for 15 minutes, he had never mentioned that in 11 previous interviews (eight with the FBI and three with defense attorneys). The defense will claim McVeigh never left the store, which means someone else had to have placed the call to Elliott's.

Defense attorneys also will challenge the eyewitnesses at Elliott's Body Shop. The initial descriptions that were provided by shop owner Eldon Elliott, employee Vicki Beemer and mechanic Tom Kessinger didn't match McVeigh's height, weight, and eye color, the defense will argue. The defense will search for a way to mention Kessinger's criminal past, especially his four-year prison term for conspiracy to manufacture PCP and methamphetamine.

It was Elliott and Kessinger who provided the now-infamous description of "John Doe 2." They initially said a second person—described as a heavyset, brown-eyed, dark-haired, muscular white man wearing a white cap with blue stripes—came in with McVeigh to rent the truck on April 17. That led to a months-long FBI manhunt for this second suspect. Last January, the government refashioned the story, conceding that Kessinger

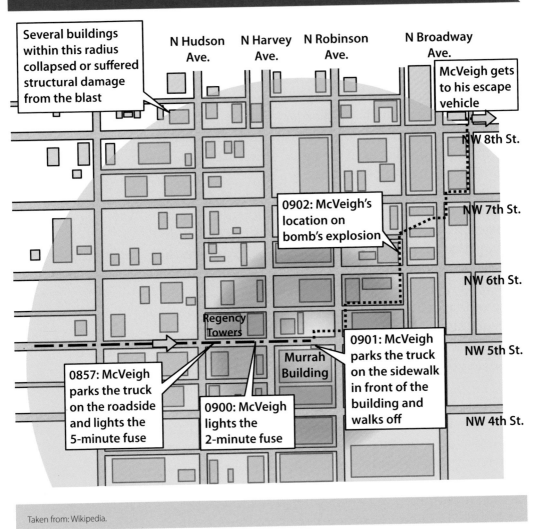

TIMOTHY MCVEIGH'S MOVEMENTS DURING THE OKLAHOMA CITY BOMBING

Several buildings within this radius collapsed or suffered structural damage from the blast

N Hudson Ave.

N Harvey Ave.

N Robinson Ave.

N Broadway Ave.

McVeigh gets to his escape vehicle

NW 8th St.

0902: McVeigh's location on bomb's explosion

NW 7th St.

NW 6th St.

Regency Towers

Murrah Building

0901: McVeigh parks the truck on the sidewalk in front of the building and walks off

NW 5th St.

0857: McVeigh parks the truck on the roadside and lights the 5-minute fuse

0900: McVeigh lights the 2-minute fuse

NW 4th St.

Taken from: Wikipedia.

was confused, and contending that John Doe 2 was actually Fort Riley Army Pvt. Todd Bunting, who had stopped by Elliott's a day later.

The defense can ask: If Kessinger was confused about John Doe 2, why should we believe him when he talks about Timothy McVeigh? The defense will float the idea that the person thought to be McVeigh was actually Army Sgt. Michael Hertig, who accompanied Bunting to Elliott's on the 18th. Hertig resembles the initial FBI sketch as much as McVeigh, Jones says, but the prosecution counters that Hertig sported an ample moustache at the time, and he didn't look like the composite at all.

Conspiracy Theory

There's a bigger conspiracy. Jones will use the mystery of John Doe 2 to make jurors wonder whether the FBI failed to pursue the real conspirators. "The government quit investigating this case a year ago," says Jones. "The FBI had a number of leads they just did not pursue." At a hearing last fall, Jones said "we certainly will contend that there is a John Doe 2, and maybe 3, 4, and 5."

On that front, he's got considerable backup, because a number of witnesses claim McVeigh and Nichols were accompanied by others on more than a few occasions. A man who delivered Chinese food to McVeigh's room at the Dreamland Motel said that someone else answered the door. A handful of witnesses claim to have seen McVeigh and the Ryder truck in downtown Oklahoma City the morning of the bombing, but most say McVeigh was joined by anywhere from one to four other people. That's why the government won't call these witnesses.

Jurors will most likely hear about a man named Robert Jacques, who, according to a CNN report, may have accompanied McVeigh and Nichols on a 1994 sojourn to look at land for sale in Missouri's Ozark Mountains. The FBI has made a sketch of a dark-featured Jacques, who has been described as perhaps Indian or Hawaiian. A senior federal law enforcement official, who doubts Jacques's existence, says he is nonetheless nagged by the number of people who have said that McVeigh was escorted by someone they described as being dark complected, swarthy, foreign or Indian—"and we've never located a person of that description."

Jones will evoke an even larger conspiracy involving domestic and foreign terrorists. In a hearing a year ago, he requested access to government intelligence data to "show that the Oklahoma City bombing . . . was planned, financed and executed by a foreign state or terrorist group under the control of a foreign state and probably in connection with a domestic terrorist organization."

Exactly where Jones is headed is difficult to pin down, but there is likely to be some mention of Elohim City, a 240-acre religious compound in the foothills of northeast Oklahoma that is home to what investigators say is a community of white supremacists. McVeigh placed a call to Elohim City two weeks before the bombing and may have been looking for a former German soldier named Andreas Strassmeir, who met McVeigh at a 1993 Tulsa gun show and was a sometime resident of Elohim City.

That's significant because a government informant had claimed that Strassmeir and a white supremacist named Dennis Mahon had discussed blowing up the Murrah building in November or December of 1994. The informant, Carol Howe, had been working with the Treasury Department's Bureau of Alcohol, Tobacco, and Firearms. She has a few credibility problems that the prosecution will undoubtedly point out. The ATF had dropped Howe as an informant four to six weeks before the bombing because she was allegedly erratic and unreliable. This month she was indicted on unrelated charges. Mahon and Strassmeir—now back in Germany—have vehemently denied any link to the bombing of the Murrah building.

Jones has been literally searching the globe for information about a worldwide conspiracy. Clocks in his office reception area display the time in London, Jerusalem, and Hong Kong. Members of the defense team have traveled to Europe, the Middle East, and especially the Philippines, "because most of the major Middle Eastern powers that are antagonistic to the United States have intelligence operations there," says Jones. He has sought government intelligence related to Iraq, Iran, and Sudan, and connections between American terrorist organizations and groups in Germany and the United Kingdom.

Conspiracy theorists will particularly delight in this "coincidence": Terry Nichols spent eight weeks visiting his wife in Cebu City, Philippines, in late 1994 and early 1995, and also made calls from Kansas phone booths to several numbers there. During much of the same time frame, the Philippines was also home to Ramzi Ahmed Yousef, who is scheduled to go on trial later this year for allegedly masterminding the World Trade Center bombing. Yousef was convicted last fall of planting a bomb on a Philippines Airlines jet bound for Tokyo in late 1994; Yousef got off that plane in Cebu City.

> The more alternative theories Jones spins, the more likely he is to convince a juror or two that the FBI may have the wrong man, or at a minimum that McVeigh is merely a pawn in a larger game.

Justice Department sources say that the alleged links to other shadowy groups are diversions. But the more alternative theories Jones spins, the more likely he is to convince a juror or two that the FBI may have the wrong man, or at minimum that McVeigh is merely a pawn in a larger game. That could set Jones's client free—or at least save him from an execution.

Notes

1. After a fifty-day siege on David Koresh's Branch Davidian compound near Waco, Texas, federal law enforcement agents opened fire on April 19, 1993, resulting in the deaths of seventy-six people.
2. Mark Fuhrman was a Los Angeles police detective known for his involvement in the 1994 investigation and 1995 trial of O.J. Simpson for the murders of Nicole Brown Simpson and Ron Goldman. Fuhrman was later convicted of perjury for his role in the trial.

The Vice President Speaks at the Dedication of the Oklahoma City National Memorial

Al Gore

In the following remarks offered at the dedication of the Oklahoma City National Memorial, the US vice president offers a eulogy to those individuals who died in the April 19, 1995, bombing of the Murrah Federal Building. He asserts that they "paid for our freedom" with their lives. He also praises those who have survived as well as the rescue workers who worked tirelessly to find the injured. Anger and hatred demean the human spirit, he says, and he urges his listeners to replace "hate with love." He concludes noting that the memorial will be a place where visitors can go for comfort, education, and remembrance. Al Gore served as vice president under President Bill Clinton from 1993 to 2001.

SOURCE. Al Gore, "Remarks Delivered by Vice President Al Gore: Oklahoma City National Memorial Dedication," clinton2.nara.gov, October 25, 1998. www.nara.gov.

Today, in the dark shadow of memory, we gather to seek the light. To find in this soil, nourished with a million tears, the harvest of God's healing grace.

For I believe in the words of the scripture: "that the sufferings of this present time are not worthy to be compared with the glory which shall be revealed in us."

The people who died here were victims of one of the cruelest visitations of evil this nation has ever seen. But we offer them today not pity, but *honor*—for as much as any soldier who ever fought in any war—they paid the price of our freedom.

> The people who died here were victims of one of the cruelest visitations of evil this nation has ever seen. But we offer them today not pity, but *honor.*

They were busy here that bright spring morning—processing Social Security checks, providing day care, helping families find housing, helping farmers plant their spring crops.

And to those who are ever tempted to denigrate the labor of our self-government, and demean our hardworking government employees, come here and be *silent*, and remember.

Open your eyes and your hearts and you will see that on the chain link fence all around us—filled with flowers and prayers and teddy bears—is written the real story of our democracy. This is how we feel.

A Memorial for the 168 Dead

And on this day, we build a memorial, with a seat for each of the 168 who died, because we will never forget the lives they lived.

Kimberly Clark, who was looking forward to her wedding the next Saturday. Marine Captain Randy Guzman—twenty eight years old—who led infantry in the Persian Gulf War. Antonio Cooper, Jr.—six months old—who had just learned to say his first word. Zachary Chavez, three years old—now buried near his mother's

home, so she can visit him every day. Aaron Coverdale, five and a half years old, and his brother Elijah, two and a half—whose father walked the streets with their photograph, asking: "Have you seen them?"

I have seen them today—in the love that shines through your tears. All of America has seen the children of Oklahoma City—and the men and women who died here as well, the wives and husbands; the mothers and fathers, and brothers and sisters, and co-workers and friends. And we will never forget them. Nor will we forget you, the families, survivors, and rescue workers. You have inspired us and lifted us up. And so, as we honor those who have been lost, we seek as well to lift you up to live a new day.

In the words of the poet [William Butler Yeats]:

Too long a sacrifice
Can make a stone of the heart.
O when may it suffice?
That is Heaven's part, our part
To murmur name upon name,
As a mother names her child
When sleep at last has come
On limbs that had run wild.

I am honored to have been seated today next to Clint Seidl. Clint was only in the second grade when he lost his mother Kathy in the bombing. Kathy worked for the Secret Service for more than ten years. Clint said recently: "I miss my mom a lot. I love my dad half to death. But a dad ain't a mom. She had a real nice face—and a beautiful smile. That's what I remember her by."

Clint was asked the other day if it was hard to have hope. He said: "I'm dreaming. I want to work for the Secret Service some day, just like my mom." Clint—you may be a little young to file an application, but I've got some Secret Service agents here with me, they are ready to talk to you after the ceremony.

I appreciate them even more today—as all of us appreciate those who serve in our self-government.

Clint knows what all of you are proving today—that in the wake of such deep destruction, the truest course is to not only remember the sacrifice of those who were lost, but to reach for the future that was in their hearts. If we restrain our voices from weeping and our eyes from tears, there is hope for our future.

Photo on previous page: The governor of Oklahoma, the mayor of Oklahoma City, US vice president Al Gore, and their wives lay a wreath at the site of the Alfred P. Murrah Federal Building on the one-year anniversary of the bombing. (AP Photo/ David Longstreath.)

Hope and Inspiration

We have already seen so much hope here, and so much inspiration—a community that came together in grief, and stayed together in compassion, and commitment, and love, and dedication. I saw it just weeks after the bombing, when Tipper and I met with Federal rescue workers here.

One police captain working the disaster received a bag of candy from a little girl called Melia. When he opened it up, he found, along with the candy, a dollar and fifteen cents—and a note thanking him for his help.

Then there was the grief counselor who emerged from ten hours of sitting with grieving families to find that he'd left a light on in his car and it would not start. A couple approached him and offered to bring their car around to give him a jump-start. The counselor then recognized the man: less than an hour earlier, he learned he had lost his two little children. The man pulled the photo of his children from his breast pocket and said: "We're all in this together."

Let there be no doubt: for those who would murder our families and our future, there must be swift and certain justice. The perpetrators of this hateful act gained nothing for their evil cause—but they turned wives into widows, and children into orphans. They brought bitter, unbearable grief to the American family. Mark my words: we will see that justice is done. We will insist on the ultimate penalty for this ultimate crime.

> From this day forward, the memory of this tragedy will live in our minds and hearts, and in the memorial we dedicate today.

What happened here put this entire nation on notice that the threat of terrorism is indeed real. It is a threat not just from without, but from within. It is a challenge for our national government—which is why President [Bill]Clinton and I worked across party lines, with your delegation and others, to win an almost $3 billion increase in funds to fight terrorism in our new budget.

A Challenge

And it is also a challenge for each one of us: to recognize that careless words and bitter emotions breed the worst in the human spirit. We must seek to replace meanness with meaning—hate with love—ugliness with grace.

That is what you have sought in raising up this memorial—to build where others have torn down. To offer strength where others preyed on the vulnerable. To find, in the empty rows of chairs that will cover this ground, a way to refill our souls and our spirits. Your work here is a great testament to our faith and striving. Oklahoma City has come together, once again, to choose hope—and that is a blessing for our entire nation. We thank you for what you mean to all of us.

Over the past three and a half years, for all who mourn the good and decent Americans lost here, this place has served as their memorial, powerful and spontaneous—attracting those who care, not only from all parts of our nation, but from all across the world.

And I believe it should continue to comfort, to educate, to illuminate for generations to come. I am proud to announce that a piece of the Murrah Building, provided at my request by the Oklahoma City National Memorial Foundation, will be placed in the permanent collection of our nation's Smithsonian Institution. This sanctified stone will be in our nation's museum, among our nation's most treasured and honored artifacts. Now, from this day forward, the memory of this tragedy will live in our minds and hearts, and in the memorial we dedicate today.

For I do believe, with all my heart, that there is hope in this place, like flowers that push through winter's barren soil.

As the old hymn suggests:

Come ye disconsolate, wher-e'er ye languish
Come to the mercy seat, fervently kneel!
Here bring your wounded hearts,
Here tell your anguish:
Earth has no sorrows that Heaven cannot heal.

Timothy McVeigh Is Sentenced to Death by a Federal Jury

Jo Thomas

The following excerpt from a newspaper article reports that on June 13, 1997, Timothy McVeigh was sentenced to death for the bombing of the Alfred P. Murrah Federal Building in Oklahoma City. The author details the factors the jury considered in reaching their recommendation. The defense presented witnesses who testified to McVeigh's happy childhood and his service in the army. The prosecution presented McVeigh as a cold-blooded killer and presented witnesses who were survivors of the attack. Although the jury found that McVeigh had no previous criminal record, he was a decorated US Army veteran, and that he served his country well, they also found that he transported explosives across state lines and intended to cause the deaths of many people. Jo Thomas led

---

SOURCE. Jo Thomas, "The Oklahoma City Bombing: the Verdict; McVeigh Jury Decides on Sentence of Death in Oklahoma City Bombing," *New York Times*, June 14, 1997, p. 1. Copyright © 1997 The New York Times Company. All rights reserved. Reproduced by permission.

the *New York Times* investigation of the Oklahoma City bombing, later serving as a professor at the S.I. Newhouse School of Public Communication at Syracuse University.

A Federal jury today voted unanimously that Timothy J. McVeigh, a 29-year-old former soldier, should be sentenced to death for the bombing of the Federal Building in Oklahoma City on April 19, 1995, which took 168 lives and injured 850 other people.

Mr. McVeigh sat quietly, his chin resting on his hands, as Judge Richard P. Matsch read the jury's decision and announced that it was final. Then the judge said he would impose the death sentence at a later hearing.

Mr. McVeigh's parents, William McVeigh and Mildred Frazer, watched silently from the front row, with their younger daughter, Jennifer, 23, between them.

> The jury . . . took slightly more than 11 hours to reach a decision on his penalty.

An audible gasp arose from the families of the victims in the back of the courtroom when the jury's decision was announced. One woman broke into tears, and another smiled broadly, but most of the relatives looked serious and grim.

The jury of seven men and five women, which convicted Mr. McVeigh of murder and conspiracy charges on June 2, took slightly more than 11 hours to reach a decision on his penalty.

Richard Burr, a defense lawyer, said Mr. McVeigh spent the morning "reading correspondence, sitting quietly, getting ready for the next phase of his life." Robert Nigh Jr., another defense lawyer, said Mr. McVeigh had reacted calmly to the jury's decision.

When Mr. McVeigh, wearing a plain gray sweatshirt, left the courtroom with the marshals, he turned, looked back at his family and silently mouthed some words.

Mrs. Frazer, interviewed afterward by Barbara Walters of ABC News, expressed anger at her son's conviction and death sentence. "For two years now, since my son—the day he was arrested—I feel that—it was done—that he was convicted and sentenced to death by the media and the Government."

The bombing was the worst terrorist act on American soil and shook the nation's sense of security within its borders. For days after, Americans were riveted by scenes of the devastation and rescue effort unfolding live on television.

"Justice prevails," Joseph H. Hartzler, the lead prosecutor, said as he left the courthouse. "The verdict doesn't diminish the great sadness that occurred in Oklahoma City two years ago. Our only hope is that the verdict will go some way to preventing such a terrible, drastic crime from ever occurring again."

Stephen Jones, the lead lawyer for Mr. McVeigh, said, "The jury has spoken, and their verdict is entitled to respect, and all Americans should afford it that respect until such time, if ever, it is overturned by a court of competent jurisdiction."

Ralph Duke, 65, who lost his daughter, Claudette Meek, 43, in the bombing, said he would have been satisfied with a life sentence but now would like to attend Mr. McVeigh's execution. "I hope it happens before I pass away," Mr. Duke said. "I'd go to his execution."

With today's verdict, Mr. McVeigh becomes the 14th Federal prisoner sentenced to death since the Federal death penalty was reinstated in 1988. But he is likely to have many years of appeals ahead of him and a long wait for execution. No Federal prisoner has been put to death since 1963.

The Jury's Task

In its case against Mr. McVeigh, the Federal Government said he had gathered the materials for a giant bomb;

rented a large Ryder truck in Junction City, Kan.; drove the truck and the bomb to Oklahoma City, and then blew up the Federal Building. The Government has also charged Terry L. Nichols, an Army friend of Mr. McVeigh, in the bombing; Mr. Nichols will be tried later.

Before they could decide that Mr. McVeigh should die, the jurors had to find that he intended to cause death, and they had to weigh aggravating factors, any of which could serve as grounds for the death penalty, against mitigating factors, presented by his defense lawyers, that he should live.

In their findings delivered to Judge Matsch today at 3:20 P.M., the jurors agreed unanimously that Mr. McVeigh acted with criminal intent to cause death. The jurors also agreed unanimously on statutory aggravating factors, including that he transported explosives across a state line while committing the crime, and was out to kill, and did kill, one or more Federal law enforcement officers.

The jurors agreed unanimously on three of the mitigating factors submitted by defense lawyers, including that Mr. McVeigh believed that the Bureau of Alcohol, Tobacco and Firearms and the Federal Bureau of Investigation were responsible for the deaths at the Branch Davidian compound near Waco, Tex., in 1993, and that he believed that "the increasing use of military-style force and tactics by Federal law enforcement agencies against American citizens threatened an approaching police state."

All 12 jurors acknowledged that Mr. McVeigh had no criminal record and that he received the Bronze Star for his service with the Army in Operation Desert Storm in Kuwait and Iraq. Ten jurors agreed he served honorably and with great distinction in the Army, from May 1988 until December 1991. But none of them agreed that he "believed deeply in the ideals upon which the United States was founded."

A newspaper clipping announcing the death penalty for Timothy McVeigh was attached alongside other mementos on a fence surrounding the remains of the Murrah Federal Building. (AP Photo/J. Pat Carter.)

None agreed that he "is a good and loyal friend." Only one said he "is a person who deals honestly with others in interpersonal relations," and two said he "is a reliable and dependable person in work and in his personal affairs and relations with others."

Under Federal law, the jurors' decision today is called a recommendation, but it is final, Judge Matsch said today.

Before he dismissed the jurors, Judge Matsch thanked them for their service. He then lifted the order forbidding the lawyers from talking to the press about the case and acknowledged the right of the jurors, now that the trial is over, to discuss the case with others. But he asked them not to comment about Mr. McVeigh's co-defendant, Mr. Nichols.

One juror, Martha B. Hite of Denver, said in a brief telephone interview this afternoon, "It was a privilege to work on this jury and for me to be a part of this jury."

Another juror, David Gilger, told The Associated Press, "I think there's a sense of closure for everyone."

President [Bill] Clinton declined to comment on the jury finding but thanked the jurors for their service and for the "grave decisions" they made in the trial. "This investigation and trial have confirmed our country's faith in its justice system," he said in a written statement.

The National Conference of Catholic Bishops issued a statement expressing "regret" that the jury chose a death sentence over life imprisonment.

Judge Matsch told the jurors today: "It may be a matter for you now or at some later time to wonder: Did we do the right thing? The answer to that question is yes, you did the right thing. Not because I believe it one way or the other, but because you did it. And that is what we rely upon: 12 people coming together, hearing the evidence, following the law and reaching the decision."

> McVeigh never shed a tear during heart-wrenching testimony that had men and women on the jury weeping and reaching for their handkerchiefs.

The Prosecutors' Case

Prosecutors tried the bombing like a homicide, although one motivated by Mr. McVeigh's anger against the Government. When they argued that he should receive the death penalty, they focused on the premeditation of the crime, the callousness of its execution and the devastation it wrought on its victims, living and dead.

The prosecutors did not mention the killer's apparent lack of remorse, but it seemed evident in the courtroom: Mr. McVeigh never shed a tear during heart-wrenching testimony that had men and women on the jury weeping and reaching for their handkerchiefs.

Mr. Nigh, one of Mr. McVeigh's lawyers, said Mr. McVeigh "tried to maintain his composure" during the trial. "He had done that, and I don't think he should be criticized for that aspect."

Mr. Hartzler addressed this point obliquely in his closing statement, reminding jurors of testimony from a neighbor of the McVeigh family in Pendleton, N.Y., near Buffalo, who said Mr. McVeigh choked back tears as he said goodbye to her before leaving for duty in the Persian Gulf.

Mr. Hartzler reminded the jurors that "not a single witness testified at any other time that Timothy McVeigh ever had a tear in his eye except when he was concerned about his own welfare."

Mr. Jones has been trying for almost two years to counter the portrayal of Mr. McVeigh as a cold, heartless and calculating killer, his stony expression burned on the memories of millions when he was shown on television leaving a county jail after his arrest.

Mr. McVeigh came to court in neat, casual clothing, usually khaki slacks and a long-sleeved sport shirt. He dressed like the jurors, not like the lawyers, most of whom wore dark suits.

In fact, Mr. McVeigh looked so much like the boy next door that Scott Mendeloff, a prosecutor, mentioned it in the last argument to the jurors before they found Mr. McVeigh guilty: "That fresh-faced young man over there, a mass murderer, killed 168 men, women and children, and tried to kill more."

Defense Lawyers' Argue Against Execution

During the penalty phase of the trial, which began on June 4, defense lawyers brought witnesses from Mr. McVeigh's hometown to testify that he had been a happy child with loving parents. Soldiers who served with Mr. McVeigh in the Army came to Denver from as far

Terry Lynn Nichols

In 1998, a federal jury found Terry Lynn Nichols guilty in the April 19, 1995, bombing of the Alfred P. Murrah Federal Building in Oklahoma City, Oklahoma. . . .

On May 10, 1995, Nichols was formally charged with the bombing and, three months later, both Nichols and Timothy McVeigh were indicted by a federal grand jury. The indictments were identical, charging each man with conspiracy to use a weapon of mass destruction, the use of a weapon of mass destruction, destruction by explosive, and eight counts of first-degree murder for the deaths of federal employees in the Murrah building. . . .

From that date forward, the prosecution linked Nichols to several key stages in the plot, including renting storage lockers and stealing 299 sticks of Tovex explosives, 544 blasting caps, and detonating cord from a quarry in Marion, Kansas, on October 1, 1994. Fingerprint evidence found on a receipt in Nichols's wallet confirmed that Nichols and McVeigh were together on April 13, 1995. Other circumstantial evidence connected Nichols to the robbery of a gun collector in Arkansas, which the

prosecution claimed was to fund the bombing conspiracy; the prosecution also suggested that Nichols drove McVeigh from Junction City, Kansas, to Oklahoma City on April 16, 1995, to drop off the getaway car. Nichols's wife, Marife Nichols, could not testify to his whereabouts on April 18; his former wife, Lana Padilla, testified that Nichols had left a package with her, to be opened in the event of his death while away in the Philippines. In this package, she found a letter written to McVeigh in which Nichols urged McVeigh, "Go for it!"

On December 24, 1997, the federal jury found Nichols guilty on one count of conspiracy and eight counts involuntary manslaughter. Unlike McVeigh, he was spared the sentence of death by a deadlocked jury. On June 4, 1998, U.S. District judge Richard P. Matsch sentenced Nichols to life in prison without possibility of parole, as well as to 48 years for the deaths of eight federal employees.

SOURCE. *"Terry Lynn Nichols,"* Encyclopedia of Terrorism. *Ed. Harvey W. Kushner. Thousand Oaks, CA: Sage Reference, 2003, pp. 260–261.*

away as Korea to testify that he was a dedicated soldier, the best they knew.

Mr. Jones and Mr. Burr were not permitted to argue in the penalty phase of the trial that Mr. McVeigh was innocent. Judge Matsch told them they had to accept the jury's verdict that Mr. McVeigh was guilty. So they tried to argue that although Mr. McVeigh killed 168 people, he was not simply a Charles Manson or John Wayne Gacy [convicted serial killers] writ large.

> [The defense] told the jury that Mr. McVeigh was a good man who committed evil acts out of what he saw as a noble motive: striking back at a tyrannical government.

They told the jury that Mr. McVeigh was a good man who committed evil acts out of what he saw as a noble motive: striking back at a tyrannical government that had murdered women and children near Waco, Tex., and at Ruby Ridge, Idaho. In these beliefs, Mr. Jones told the jury, Mr. McVeigh was not alone in his beliefs that the Government was out of control. There are many, he said, who agreed with him.

And in his closing argument, Mr. Jones seemed to be urging the jury not to make Mr. McVeigh a martyr to the far right by executing him. "You have to make the first step to restore domestic tranquillity," he said.

Mr. Jones also told the jury that executing Mr. McVeigh might foreclose the possibility of finding others involved in the plot. The unknown conspirators mentioned in the grand jury indictment got only the barest mention during the trial from either the prosecution or the defense, he pointed out.

Mr. Hartzler called Mr. Jones's remarks about domestic tranquillity "tantamount to almost a terrorist threat: 'Hey, ladies and gentlemen of the jury, don't give him death because other bad things may happen.' That is pure intimidation."

Turning to testimony from Mr. McVeigh's parents and childhood friends and a video shown to the jury about his youth, Mr. Hartzler said: "We do not dispute that Timothy McVeigh was a good boy, and my emphasis is on the term 'was.' He's now a man. He's changed. He's no longer the good boy that he was."

The last Federal prisoner to be put to death was Victor H. Feguer, 28, hanged in Iowa for kidnapping and killing Dr. Edward Roy Bartels, a Dubuque physician. Mr. Feguer, who wanted to die, told Federal authorities he opposed appeals.

From 1927 to 1963, the Government executed 32 men and 2 women. Federal executions stopped after 1963 as state death penalty laws were challenged as arbitrary. In 1972 the Supreme Court struck down state laws on capital punishment, and the Federal law fell by analogy.

In 1988, Congress reinstated the Federal death penalty for "drug kingpin" murders and drug-related murders of law enforcement officers. In 1994, Congress expanded the law to cover 60 offenses, including using a weapon of mass destruction, destruction by an explosive, and the murder of Federal law enforcement officers performing their duties.

Mr. McVeigh, who was convicted of each of those offenses, will die by lethal injection if the sentence is upheld. The place he would be put to death is still unknown.[1]

Note

1. Timothy McVeigh was executed by lethal injection on June 11, 2001, in Terre Haute, Indiana.

A Canadian Perspective on the Execution of Timothy McVeigh

Robert Sheppard

In the following essay, a journalist comments on the atmosphere in Terre Haute, Indiana, just two days before the scheduled execution of Timothy McVeigh for the bombing of the Murrah Federal Building in Oklahoma City. He describes the people of Terre Haute as well as those who are arriving for the event, including media people, grief counselors, death penalty abolitionists, and pro-death penalty demonstrators, among others. As a Canadian, he is shocked by the casual discussions of the death penalty, although he concedes that McVeigh seems to be a suitable candidate for the death penalty. He concludes by detailing the extraordinary precision of the planning for the event. Robert Sheppard worked as a senior editor at *Maclean's* before joining the Canadian Broadcasting Corporation as a news producer in 2006.

SOURCE. Robert Sheppard, "Anatomy of an Excecution," *Maclean's*, vol. 114, no. 20, May 14, 2001, pp. 42–45. Copyright © Maclean's. All rights reserved. Reproduced by permission.

In a dewey, verdant field in rural Indiana, a few thousand people will pass a dark spring night next week waiting for the sun to come up and a man to die. Inside an otherwise nondescript brick building a few hundred metres away, about 40 others will bear direct witness to the execution, from the four glassed-in viewing rooms at the federal penitentiary just outside this small midwestern town. Another 300 or so, family members of the 168 men, women and children Timothy McVeigh killed with a truck bomb in Oklahoma City six years ago in the worst act of terrorism on American soil, will take in his final moments on closed-circuit television at a second prison in Oklahoma. But make no mistake—although only the designated will actually see McVeigh succumb to a dose of lethal chemicals at shortly after 7 A.M. central time on Wednesday, May 16, this is a public execution of the first order. An entire nation will be watching for the final word, much of it on breakfast TV.

> Although only the designated will actually see McVeigh succumb to a dose of lethal chemicals . . . this is a public execution of the first order.

On the flowing grassy knolls that surround the prison proper, a fairgrounds-like concoction of satellite trucks, wedding-sized tents, cable trails and cellphone towers is being assembled to service nearly 1,400 members of the news media, many there for an almost week-long death-watch. Given the logistics involved, some are calling it America's first catered execution.

Just after midnight on May 16 [2001] buses will begin trucking in anywhere from a few hundred to a few thousand demonstrators—the pro-death penalty crowd and the abolitionists—to designated "processing points" (as warden Harley Lappin likes to call them) on the 33-acre prison site. The groups will be at least 500m [1,640 feet] apart, connected by makeshift trails through the fields to be travelled only by accredited media on golf carts—no more than three carts per news organization is the rule Lappin has laid down. Grief counsellors will be on hand for those family members who witness the execution; public relations officials for those who want to be guided to the media tent.

The entire event has been meticulously planned for months by at least three different federal departments and local authorities—hyper-organization creeping in where solemnity fears to tread. Leave aside for the moment the emotionally charged debate about capital punishment—Americans are more than willing to take that one on. The unspoken element of the McVeigh execution is that it is a triumph of inclusivity, where both the victims' rights movement and the mainstream press have joined those with their hands on the syringe in the formal planning. Throw in a dollop of ever-present midwestern politeness, with its constant "y'alls" and milk-fed graciousness, and what's left is a kind of McDeath, an extraordinary event made ordinary with a nod to transparency and conveyor-belt efficiency.

The Death Penalty Debate

Of course, the McVeigh execution *is* highly unusual. In recent years, with the annual number of executions in the United States creeping up into the high 90s—nearly two per week, most of them in southern states like Texas and Virginia—the death penalty has become a topic of heated discussion in many quarters. But there has never been anything like this. Across the United States, columnists and TV pundits rage about whether the 33-year-old McVeigh should die—quickly or slowly—or be forced to waste away in a federal pen, Canadian-style, so he doesn't become a martyr for his cause. "Execution's too easy for him," says the cheery lady at the checkout counter at a Terre Haute motel. "That's just exactly what he wants." One side debate: the American Society of Newspaper Editors turned aside White House pleas to tone down

The execution chamber in the federal prison in Terre Haute, Indiana, where Timothy McVeigh was put to death by lethal injection. (Scott Olson/Newsmakers/Getty Images.)

the McVeigh coverage, saying the media doesn't need a civics lesson from a President who presided over 131 executions during the five years he was governor of Texas.

And so the hype picks up its pace. All last week, local television stations broadcast home videos of McVeigh as a youngster—a Boy Scout who went bad. A court action to allow Internet and pay TV broadcast of the execution was turned down by a judge, but some public stations and the ABC TV program *Nightline* aired recently acquired audiotapes of executions that took place in Georgia between 1983 and 1998, recordings that showed all too clearly the mundane bureaucracy of a public death.

And in Terre Haute (population 59,000), ground zero of this latest drama, the good citizens have been subject to an ever-increasing drumbeat of alarm (will militia fanatics attack them for being host to this event?) and worse: constantly having to explain themselves to a descending horde of foreigners who can't understand America's fascination with capital punishment. "They say you have to play the cards you're dealt," Judy Anderson, the county commissioner for Terre Haute, said recently at a ceremony to plant 168 redbud saplings, the state tree of Oklahoma, in her county. "I know the whole situation is a necessary evil that we have to deal with."

> For the Canadian visitor, the culture shock is jarring. . . . Talk of the death penalty just seems to wash about casually in everyday discussion.

Terre Haute didn't ask to be the site of the only federal execution chamber in the United States. That was a twist of geography. In the early 1990s, when the U.S. government decided to consolidate its relative handful of federal death-row inmates (20 versus the approximately 4,000 in the individual states) in one institution, it chose the U.S. Penitentiary at Terre Haute because it was the most central federal jail in the country. The Crossroads of America, it says on Indiana licence plates. A section of the 60-year-old jail that used to house Cuban detainees was cleared out, and two years ago death-row prisoners, including its most famous, Inmate McVeigh as prison officials call him, were moved in. Coincidentally, it is only a short drive south of Terre Haute where the last public hanging in the United States took place in 1936 at Owensboro, Ky.: a boisterous crowd of 20,000 turned up to watch the execution of a black man for raping and killing an older white woman, and the ensuing revelry at the event caused the rest of the country to turn away in revulsion.

Culture Shock

For the Canadian visitor, the culture shock is jarring. It's not just the carnival atmosphere that some are bringing to the event, or the mantra you can overhear on the street: he did it, he's unrepentant, he deserves to pay the price. It's the fact that talk of the death penalty just seems to wash about casually in everyday discussion or on TV and the radio, like the price of gas.

Those who lost family in the Oklahoma City bombing—a revenge act, said McVeigh, for federal agents storming a militia compound in Waco, Tex., in 1993, where 80 people were killed—routinely pop up on both sides of the issue. Some have befriended McVeigh's father, Bill, a retired autoplant worker in Buffalo, N.Y. One women who lost two grandchildren in the blast has spent her time tracing McVeigh's footsteps in the weeks leading up to the attack—even to the point of sleeping in the same motel bed he did—researching this for a documentary. She doesn't want McVeigh executed now because she feels he may be part of a larger conspiracy that has yet to be uncovered.

Even in the darkest days of [Canadian serial killer] Paul Bernardo or child killer Clifford Olson, there was never any of this, never even any sustained public debate about the death penalty in Canada. "I certainly never heard or felt anything like this kind of emotion," observes Toronto lawyer Timothy Danson, who represented families of both Bernardo's and Olson's victims. "We're just so different from the Americans in this regard." The newest argument making the rounds is that all the publicity surrounding the McVeigh execution is justified because it will bring closure to the bereaved families of Oklahoma City—some 3,000 people in total. Although, as Danson says, "once you accept the fact that victims can watch an execution, at what point does the general public say, through the media, we have an interest in this, too? Where do you draw the line?"

For the moment, perhaps, that line is being drawn through the heart of Middle America—Terre Haute, Ind. Once a thriving river town with coal mines and heavy industry, Terre Haute is like any number of midsize Canadian cities that progress has passed by. To the east lies the rail and trucking hub that is Indianapolis, to the west, the self-proclaimed Gateway to the West, St. Louis. Terre Haute's claim to fame: the first mass production of the long-playing record album, the invention of the Coke bottle and (less apple pie-ish) the resurgence of the Ku Klux Klan in the 1920s.

Terre Haute is the kind of place where new products are taken to be tested, and as in any small community, people's reactions to something as novel as the execution of a mass murderer in their backyard run the gamut. They may even reflect the new ambivalence Americans seem to have towards the death penalty. According to a national poll last week, 63 per cent are in favour, down from a high of 80 per cent in the mid-1990s. Also, in this newest poll, support for executions drops to 46 per cent when life without parole is offered as an alternative.

Trying to make their own peace with this tragedy, Terre Haute churches of different denominations have come together to organize prayer services and vigils for both the Monday and Tuesday evenings preceding the execution. This is a churchgoing part of the world. A self-proclaimed Jesus freak purchased a billboard on the main highway to the penitentiary, urging folks to pray for Timothy McVeigh. But in what is probably a better read of the town's mood, the sign company put up two of its own billboards, urging people to pray for the 168 victims of the bombing.

Down at the Body Art tattoo parlour, co-owner Debbie Walker is making a small killing selling souvenir buttons and T-shirts. The one with the "Die! Die! Die!" logo, and a cruder version, are currently outselling the abolitionist variant by about 180 to 3. Walker offered to make a donation from each sale to the Oklahoma City memorial for the bombing victims, but was politely turned aside. Is she not concerned her neighbours might say she is profiting from a tragedy? "Are you kidding me?" she replies. "Who is not profiting from this? All the stores, the gas stations, the hotels? Don't get on me just because we thought of something new. McVeigh, he don't care. He's ruined thousands of lives."

A few blocks away, at the downtown campus of Indiana State University, political scientist Kirby Goidel and colleagues are organizing an intensive three-week course on the death penalty that will run right through the McVeigh execution. Students wanted it, so did some faculty. So far, about 20 students have signed up, which is not bad for an all-day summer course in May, says Goidel. If it helps some students deal with the strong emotions surrounding this issue, so much the better, he says. But he doesn't hold much hope for the execution itself being cathartic: "It's like knowing a car crash is going to happen. Is it really something you are going to feel good watching?" With public schools closed for the day, many families he knows are simply planning to pack up their kids and get out of town.

> The problem for liberals in Terre Haute and probably throughout America is that McVeigh is almost a poster boy for the death penalty.

The problem for liberals in Terre Haute and probably throughout America is that McVeigh is almost a poster boy for the death penalty. Politely unrepentant, he was even willing to have his death telecast. He doesn't seem to have a friend in the world. An enigmatic killer, McVeigh is almost more scary because he is so ordinary. In a profile shortly after his arrest in 1995, *The Washington Post* observed: "In deeply disturbing ways, he is a prototype of his generation." He lived through the upheaval of parental divorce when he was a young boy, the crashing job market of the early 1980s while a young man, a briefly exhilarating period in the army during the war against Saddam Hussein, and then, like so many others of his age, found himself back home as an adult, sleeping in his old room, with nowhere to go.

Warden Lappin says McVeigh has been "a very manageable individual since he's been here, and continues to be so." He made three fairly routine appeals of his conviction and then, in December, filed a motion that he would not seek another. Five weeks later, his execution date was set. In early April, his father and sister Jennifer came for their final visit. According to Bill McVeigh, his son refused to apologize to anyone for his crime and laughed off his family's request for a hug. His last words are already the subject of intense speculation. They will be made while he is strapped to the death chair, the IV in his arm but before the chemicals will have been administered. Four separate groups of witnesses and a camera will be looking on from behind darkened windows.

Planning the Execution

It is said the devil is in the details, and for the execution of Timothy McVeigh, not much has been left to chance. His last three days on earth have been planned almost to the minute. The same holds true for the assembling media, which begin setting up on the prison site eight days before the event in accordance with a meticulously drawn schedule. Also for the demonstrators: government buses will begin picking them up at two Terre Haute riverside parks at precisely 12:01 on the morning of the 16th and will run back and forth all night until the deed is done. Silent prayer vigils are planned for 4:12 A.M., precisely 168 minutes before the formal execution is to commence.

For warden Lappin, a folksy if somewhat technocratic midwesterner, this is his first execution. But he has told local groups he has been "practising," and that he has visited other states to watch how lethal injections are carried out. In a recent media briefing that went on for more than two hours, Lappin said that in his experience it usually takes between four and eight minutes for the chemicals to take effect. (Mind you, death penalty opponents have documented 32 cases of botched executions since 1982.) He said he expects to emerge "about 15 minutes" after the start time, which may not be exactly at 7 o'clock, to relay what's gone on. The imprecision was too much for some. An NBC producer who had been negotiating the media details on behalf of the networks reminded Lappin that they will all be on air live at that point—"15 minutes will be an eternity for us." It was said in a room of 200 people, without the slightest irony.

CHAPTER 2

Controversies Surrounding the Oklahoma City Bombing

McVeigh Reveals His Motives for Bombing the Federal Building

Tracy McVeigh

Photo on previous page: Law enforcement and armored vehicles search for a Hutaree Militia fugitive in Hillsdale County, Michigan, on March 29, 2010. Many blame militia groups—and the US government's response to them—for violent events such as the Oklahoma bombing. **(AP Photo/Madalyn Ruggiero.)**

In the following essay, a British reporter (no relation) reveals the contents of letters he received from Timothy McVeigh regarding his motive for bombing the Murrah Federal Building in Oklahoma City. In these letters, Timothy McVeigh claims that he committed the bombing as an act of war against an enemy, the US federal government, in response to government raids on places like Ruby Ridge, Idaho, where members of Randy Weaver's family were killed by federal agents, and Waco, Texas, where David Koresh and seventy-five of his followers died when federal law enforcement agents stormed the group's compound. The letters also assert that McVeigh undertook the bombing to put a stop to governmental abuse of power. Tracy McVeigh is a chief reporter for the *Observer*, a British newspaper.

The indepth letters Timothy McVeigh invited the *Observer* to look at were sent to the safekeeping of his friend Bob Papovich who had up until now been told that the correspondence was to be kept "off-the-record".

But in a letter to Papovich written from death row on May 3, 2001, McVeigh told Papovich that these documents he had sent him contained "the final piece missing from the 'why' equation".

In a letter to *Observer* journalist Tracy McVeigh [no relation to Timothy McVeigh], the convicted Oklahoma City bomber gave Papovich's phone number and pleaded: "Ask him specifically for my 3-page letter why I bombed the Murrah building".

The following is that letter which shows the build-up of anger that McVeigh had against a US federal government "run amok" against its citizens and the politics that led to his bombing of the Alfred P Murrah building in Oklahoma City on April 19, 1995—the second anniversary of Waco.[1]

The First Letter from Timothy McVeigh

What McVeigh wrote:

I explain herein why I bombed the Murrah federal building in Oklahoma City. I explain this not for publicity, nor seeking to win an argument of right or wrong. I explain so that the record is clear as to my thinking and motivations in bombing a government installation.

I chose to bomb a federal building because such an action served more purposes than other options. Foremost the bombing was a retaliatory strike; a counter attack for the cumulative raids (and subsequent violence and damage) that federal agents had participated in over the preceding years (including, but not limited to, Waco). From the formation of such units as the FBI's Hostage Rescue and other assault teams amongst federal

agencies during the 80s, culminating in the Waco incident, federal actions grew increasingly militaristic and violent, to the point where at Waco, our government—like the Chinese—was deploying tanks against its own citizens.

Knowledge of these multiple and ever-more aggressive raids across the country constituted an identifiable pattern of conduct within and by the federal government and amongst its various agencies.

For all intents and purposes, federal agents had become soldiers (using military training, tactics, techniques, equipment, language, dress, organisation and mindset) and they were escalating their behaviour.

Therefore this bombing was meant as a pre-emptive (or pro-active) strike against these forces and their command and control centres within the federal building. When an aggressor force continually launches attacks from a particular base of operations, it is sound military strategy to take the fight to the enemy. Additionally, borrowing a page from US foreign policy, I decided to send a message to a government that was becoming increasingly hostile, by bombing a government building and the government employees within that building who represent that government. Bombing the Murrah federal building was morally and strategically equivalent to the US hitting a government building in Serbia, Iraq, or other nations.

Based on observations of the policies of my own government, I viewed this action as an acceptable option.

From this perspective, what occurred in Oklahoma City was no different than what Americans rain on the heads of others all the time, and subsequently, my mindset was and is one of clinical detachment. (The bombing of the Murrah building was not personal, no more than when Air Force, Army, Navy or Marine personnel bomb or launch cruise missiles against government installations and their personnel). I hope that this clarification amply addresses all questions.

> 'I decided to send a message to a government that was becoming increasingly hostile, by bombing a government building and the government employees within that building.'

Photo on previous page: Fire consumed the Branch Davidian cult compound in Waco, Texas, after an FBI raid on April 19, 1993. Seventy-six cult members were killed. (**Mark Perlstein/ Time Life Pictures/Getty Images.**)

A Second Letter from McVeigh

Another letter sent to Papovich stated:

> When the post-inferno investigations and inquiries by the Executive and Legislative branches of government concluded that the federal government had done nothing fundamentally wrong during the raid of the Branch Davidians at Waco, the system not only failed the victims who died during that siege but also failed the citizens of this country. This failure in effect left the door open for more Wacos.

McVeigh went on to the window of opportunity for federal agents to be held accountable for their crimes against "we the people". [That window] was again slammed shut during the court process when the US courts held that federal agents were not accountable for "the massive loss of lives and property as well as an absolute denial of due process".

> Some time after the fact they received awards, bonus pay and in some cases promotions for their disgusting and inhumane actions at Waco and Ruby Ridge.[2]
>
> This was exemplified years later while I sat in prison. The Ruby Ridge FBI sniper, Lon Horiuchi, was charged by the state of Idaho for his actions.
>
> The federal courts threw out the charges, ruling that federal agents are immune from the laws that govern the common citizen.
>
> The surviving Davidians were sentenced to lengthy prison terms, despite protests from the trial jurors. The primary "checks and balances" system had again failed to correct the system.
>
> It was at this time, after waiting for non-violent checks and balances to correct ongoing federal abuses and seeing no such results, that the assault weapons ban was passed and rumours subsequently surfaced of nationwide, Waco-style raids scheduled for the spring of

Waco: April 19, 1993

On February 28, 1993, the Bureau of Alcohol, Tobacco and Firearms (ATF) raided the Branch Davidian compound in Waco, Texas. Neighbors of the religious group complained of hearing machine-gun fire and a United Parcel Service employee reported delivering two cases of hand grenades and black gunpowder (discovered accidentally when the package tore). Members of the cult who had defected in previous months also alleged child abuse by some of the cult's members. The ATF, concerned about the possible illegal firearm activity, initiated a surprise raid on the compound. Forty-five minutes before the raid, a federal agent who had infiltrated the group reported that David Koresh, the cult's leader, received a phone call warning him that the bureau was on its way. The agent sneaked out of the compound and warned the bureau that the surprise raid was impossible, but the bureau decided to continue the raid anyway. After ninety-one agents had arrived at the compound, one federal agent approached the open front door with a search warrant. The door was slammed shut and gunfire immediately followed. Four federal agents and six cult members were killed in the shootout and sixteen more agents were wounded. Both groups blamed the other for firing first. The botched raid began a stand-off that ended fifty-one days later in the fiery deaths of all Davidians who remained inside the compound.

1995 to confiscate firearms.

These rumours were so persistent and deemed so credible that some congresswoman wrote letters to Attorney-General Janet Reno inquiring as to her intents and admonishing her to call off the raids.

As it turns out these rumours were actually based on fact.

Ruby Ridge: August 21–22, 1992

Ruby Ridge, Idaho, was the site of a 1992 incident that fueled several subsequent acts of antigovernment terrorism in the United States. On August 21 and 22, 1992, federal authorities engaged in a shoot-out with members of a Christian fundamentalist family whose head, Randy Weaver, had moved his wife and children to a remote wilderness area to avoid government interference.

The groundwork for the shoot-out was laid when, in 1989, Randy Weaver sold illegal firearms unknowingly to undercover agents of the US Bureau of Alcohol, Tobacco and Firearms (ATF). Weaver had originally met these men at a meeting of a group called Aryan Nations, and after his arrest for illegal weapons sales, the ATF asked him to work undercover as an informant on the activities of this group and other militants. Weaver not only refused but, while out on bail, failed to show up for his first court date. Federal agents consequently began a surveillance of his compound at Ruby Ridge. Instead, Weaver's son Sam spotted three of the agents while patrolling the grounds with his dog and another man, Kevin Harris. A shoot-out ensued, and Sam and the dog were killed, along with a US marshal, William Degan. The federal government then sent additional forces into the area, some of whom were part of the US Hostage Rescue Team

(HRT). Shortly thereafter, an HRT sniper fired into the house, killing Weaver's wife, Vicki, and wounding Harris, and one week later, those still alive in the house surrendered to authorities.

Weaver was tried and found innocent of all charges related to illegal weaponry, though he was found guilty of failing to appear for his original court date. Meanwhile the US Congress launched an investigation into the actions of federal agents at Ruby Ridge, and in the end they condemned those agents for the way they had handled the situation, though they also found Weaver partially responsible because he had created the circumstances of the shoot-out by avoiding his court date.

Many right-wing extremists, particularly members of the antigovernment Patriot and Christian Identity movements, considered the Ruby Ridge incident as proof that the US government was planning to end democracy and eliminate personal freedoms. As a result, some of these extremists cited Ruby Ridge as their reason for committing terrorist acts; such was the case, for example, with Timothy McVeigh, who bombed the Alfred P. Murrah Federal Building in Oklahoma City, Oklahoma, in 1995.

Through the legal process called "discovery" the Oklahoma City bombing defence learned that both the ATF (Bureau of Alcohol, Tobacco and Firearms) and the FBI had formulated raid plans for the spring of 1995 at Elohim City in eastern Oklahoma. So for those who dismiss such concerns as paranoia you need to look at the facts as they existed at the time and further reflect that the Waco raid was not imaginary—it was a real event.

> 'I reached the decision to go on the offensive—to put a check on government abuse of power where others had failed.'

It was in this climate then, that I reached the decision to go on the offensive—to put a check on government abuse of power where others had failed in stopping the federal juggernaut run amok.

Notes

1. On April 19, 1993, federal law enforcement officers began an assault on David Koresh's Branch Davidian compound near Waco, Texas. Seventy-six people died.
2. A 1992 incident at Ruby Ridge, Idaho, between Randy Weaver and his family and federal agents resulted in the deaths of Weaver's son and wife and US marshall William Degan.

McVeigh's Defense Attorney Says His Client's Confession Is a Lie

Stephen Jones

In the following essay, Timothy McVeigh's defense attorney asserts that McVeigh lied when he confessed that he was solely responsible for the Oklahoma City bombing. According to the lawyer, McVeigh did not want to share the credit with anyone else. However, he further asserts that McVeigh told him that there was another person involved, the so-called John Doe No. 2. Although the lawyer believes that there was sufficient evidence to find McVeigh guilty, he also believes that McVeigh did not receive a fair trial and has reasonable doubt that McVeigh committed murder. All of the truth did not come out regarding John Doe No. 2 and a greater conspiracy, because McVeigh claimed that he himself was the only perpetrator. Stephen Jones is an attorney in

Oklahoma and served as Timothy McVeigh's lead defense lawyer during the Oklahoma City bombing trial.

O nly a few weeks before Timothy McVeigh's scheduled execution, a new book was released with all the attendant hype and promotion and the demonizing media-driven sensationalism that have characterized the Oklahoma City bombing case since the first images of Tim McVeigh were telecast to the nation on April 21, 1995. Written by two Buffalo, New York police reporters [Lou Michel and Dan Herbeck] and based on seventy-five hours of interviews with the condemned man, *American Terrorist: Timothy McVeigh and the Oklahoma City Bombing* purported to contain Tim's last and full confession—"complete, candid and no-holds-barred."

> Unfortunately, Tim [McVeigh]'s last 'confession' was untrue.

And so it did, in a way. It was also Tim's final, but very vintage manipulation—of the world and of himself, his last-ditch effort to grab the microphone of history and transmit a heroic and very simple message: "Look at what one determined man can do."

McVeigh's "Confession"

Unfortunately, Tim's last "confession" was untrue. But it also, as I shall explain, liberated me from the strictures our legal system imposes on any lawyer, and which is called lawyer-client privilege. I am now, for better and for worse, free to tell all.

I was Tim McVeigh's lead defender, an Oklahoma lawyer, court-appointed. I fought for two years to defend him against the grand jury's indictment—defend him, that is, not only against his Department of Justice prosecutors and in the court of public opinion, but, as I shall also explain, against himself. . . .

Stephen Jones, a former attorney for Timothy McVeigh, talks to the media in front of the Oklahoma City Memorial after the announcement of the thirty-day stay of execution for McVeigh. (Jerry Laizure/Getty Images.)

I cannot in all conscience leave the last word on this most terrible and most human tragedy to Tim McVeigh, its self-styled perpetrator, or to the two journalists who in *American Terrorist* have served as his messenger. If the main thrust and narrative of my own book remain the same—it still tells the story of why our own Department of Justice fought so long and so hard to keep so many of the facts of the Oklahoma bombing from ever being aired—I have now filled in the blanks.

Tim McVeigh and his chief prosecutor, Joe Hartzler, who publicly stated that he wanted to send Tim to hell, had one thing in common to which they held with an unshakeable tenacity. Both publicly professed that Tim McVeigh was primarily responsible for the bombing and the 168 deaths that occurred in Oklahoma City on April

19, 1995. Both wanted desperately to say that McVeigh was *solely* responsible, but they couldn't quite get there.

Either way, both were wrong. And either way, both knew they were wrong.

Tim McVeigh wanted to believe it in part because, as he once told me, "If no one else is arrested or convicted, then the revolution can continue." He was convinced that in fifty years he would be seen as a hero, not unlike the men who had lived and died for our independence in the Revolutionary War. Tim could and did cite the Declaration of Independence from memory. He honestly believed that one day a statue commemorating him would be erected on the Mall in Washington, D.C. between the U.S. Capitol Building and the Washington Monument. He consistently describes himself not as a martyr but as a patriot.

> [McVeigh] wanted to go down in history as the one who had struck by stealth at the heart of government and had wreaked destruction and loss of life on an unimagined and unprecedented level.

He also wanted the limelight, the credit. All the credit. He saw himself as the avenger. The old Chevy Geo he drove, until it gave out a few months before the bombing, he called the "Road Warrior." He wanted to go down in history as the one who had struck by stealth at the heart of government and had wreaked destruction and loss of life on an unimagined and unprecedented level. As for the loss of life, he viewed it as "collateral damage." Innocent civilians are killed in every war, he told me, and April 19, 1995, in Oklahoma City—the 220th anniversary of the Battle of Concord as well as the second anniversary of the Battle of Waco[1]—was but another day in the ongoing struggle.

McVeigh Manipulated the Media

Tim McVeigh wasn't dumb—not in the slightest—although it infuriated him when people thought he was.

He could be very friendly, and he was intelligent, also manipulative, also cunning. From the first day I met him, on May 8, 1995, he worked purposefully to secure his place in history and, through his lies, to protect others who would survive his death. He used whatever tools at hand to this end. He even tried to use me, and sometimes he succeeded.

I will cite but one example among many. On May 17, 1995—that is, less than a month after the bombing and nine days after I had met Tim—a two-column front-page story by Pam Belluck appeared in the *New York Times* that began: "Timothy J. McVeigh has claimed responsibility for the Oklahoma City bombing, according to two people who have talked with him in jail since his arrest."

The story became an international sensation. It was picked up almost everywhere over the next forty-eight hours. What's more, it was dead-on accurate. Most people, of course, assumed that McVeigh had confided what he'd done to fellow prisoners, who had then passed it on to the media, and neither the *Times* nor the defense saw fit to correct them. But the truth was that the source of the "jailhouse confession" was Tim McVeigh, who instructed me to talk to the *New York Times* on a background basis for reasons I will detail later. The two people who had talked with Tim in jail were none other than myself and an associate.

Unfortunately, the authors of *American Terrorist* believed Tim when he told them, four years later, that I leaked the story because I "craved the nationwide publicity the case had brought me." The truth is that I did so because my client ordered me to. I have sitting before me now, as I write, a handwritten, two-page memo, signed and initialed "TJM" next to every paragraph, expressly authorizing me to "talk off the record and on background to NY Times," regarding, among other items, Tim's responsibility for the bombing. . . .

As to why Tim wanted this, that is another story, one I can now tell. And I will in due course.

Stuck with John Doe No. 2

Joe Hartzler was different. Hard to like. Even his own colleagues kept their distance from him, and some actively disliked him. But he had an almost impossible task. The Department of Justice had evidence, very early, that others besides McVeigh and Terry Nichols had participated in the bombing. It should be remembered that the indictment they asked the grand jury for, and got, was against Timothy McVeigh, Terry Nichols, and Others Unknown, which became the title of this book. Soon after Harzler came into the case, he was stuck with "others unknown." He had James Nichols, Terry's brother, at the head of a list of suspects for the bombing and possibly enough evidence to indict him, but not enough admissible evidence to convict. He had Michael and Lori Fortier, active members of the conspiracy, but they were allowed to plea bargain. Another conspirator was dead before McVeigh was even arrested, and two or three others got lost in the mists of time and possibly a flawed investigation.

And he—Hartzler—was stuck with John Doe #2. Early in the case, the elusive John Doe #2 was the subject of a national manhunt. For a while, the government thought they had him identified in the person of a GI, one Todd Bunting, but Todd Bunting, it turned out, had an ironclad alibi for the two key days in which witnesses claimed to have identified

> There was indeed a John Doe #2. I knew it from an unimpeachable source. Tim McVeigh.

him. As I shall relate, not only did the government abandon Todd Bunting as a suspect, but a year and a half later, at a pre-trial hearing before Judge Matsch, they used him as "proof" that John Doe #2 had never existed! Another suspect also had a name—Robert Jacques—but the government could never find him. Subsequently the hapless Hartzler was left defending the proposition that there were no other conspirators besides Nichols and McVeigh, and, to a lesser extent, the Fortiers. In other words, the way the prosecution's case evolved, "others unknown" had been a mistake. Others unknown had never existed.

As I will now make clear, there was indeed a John Doe #2.

I knew it from an unimpeachable source.

Tim McVeigh.

Stuck with Tim McVeigh

But just as Joe Harzler is stuck with John Doe #2, at least in the eyes of history, so was I stuck with my client. As I told Tim early in the case, "I do not represent your personality, your political views, or your friends or fellow conspirators. I represent you, Tim, and my duty is to protect your legal interests. Until such time as you tell me that you are willing to stand up and plead guilty, then I am required by my oath of office to do and say everything that I can for you, within the limits permitted me by my oath as an attorney, to secure your acquittal."

In truth, Judge Matsch would never in a million years have allowed Tim to change his plea to guilty on Tim's terms, even had Tim agreed. But in a confidential memo my associate, Mike Roberts, wrote after a conversation with Tim on December 4, 1996, "Tim has told me he has the following four objectives at trial: 1) that the truth of the bombing come out; 2) that he be acquitted; 3) that he embarrass the government; 4) that after all the evidence is heard, the case remains a mystery."

Strange to say, I, Tim's lawyer, knew that these seemingly contradictory objectives were not mutually exclusive. I believed that if the truth came out—the *whole* truth—then Tim would be acquitted of at least the capital charges, and that his acquittal would indeed embarrass the government, and, finally, that aspects of the case would remain a mystery.

The whole truth?

Let me phrase it this way. It is very hard for a lawyer in a criminal case to defend a guilty man whom the state can prove is guilty. I know, because I have done it many times. It is just as hard, I would say, to defend an innocent man whom the state can prove is guilty. But to defend a man who claims he is guilty—in unison with the state and the public—when a considerable body of evidence suggests that he is not guilty, that perhaps is the lawyer's greatest challenge of all.

The United States v. Timothy J. McVeigh in my judgment falls into the latter category.

I set out to find the whole truth. I did so despite the federal government's efforts to conceal it but in the face of my own client's insistence on blocking me at every turn. I did so at great expense—somewhere between $15 and $20 million of taxpayers' money—not because I sought to enrich myself (if so, I failed egregiously), but because I believed with all my heart and mind that my client, no matter how unwilling, no matter how heinous the crime of which he was accused, deserved the best defense I could possibly offer him. . . .

McVeigh Did Not Receive a Fair Trial

We went to trial in the spring of 1997. I now concede, for the first time, that there was sufficient evidence presented to the jury and known to me that painted Tim McVeigh as a member of the conspiracy to bomb and destroy the Alfred P. Murrah Federal Building. But Tim, I resolutely maintain, did not receive a fair trial. More importantly, there remains significant reasonable doubt, in my mind, as to whether he himself committed murder.

The jury, needless to say, didn't agree with me, nor did the general public, which appears to have welcomed the verdicts. Nor finally—for reasons that will now become very clear—did Tim. So be it. True to himself, Tim sought to maintain control of his fate to the very end. It was Tim who cut off the appeals process, Tim who asked that a date be set as early as possible for his execution. Once the two Buffalo journalists' book came out, and through their medium he got to proclaim his own version of the truth, there was presumably nothing left for him to do but die.

Barring some unforeseen eleventh-hour event, Tim McVeigh will be dead by lethal injection . . . in the federal prison in Terre Haute, Indiana. We already know that the media, ever true to themselves, will have turned the event into a full-fledged carnival. According to a vice-president of CBS News, it already has a name: "Deathwatch." This too may be what Tim wanted, although, much as I shudder to think it, he might well have preferred that the injection itself be witnessed on international TV.

Better demonization than oblivion.

To borrow from Winston Churchill, the Oklahoma City bombing is a mystery wrapped in an enigma inside a riddle, and so it may always remain. But it is also likely to remain one of the significant events of our troubled times. For this reason above all, now that my former client has made his own last contribution to the historical record, I am compelled to do likewise.

Note

1. On April 19, 1993, federal law enforcement officers began an assault on David Koresh's Branch Davidian compound near Waco, Texas. Seventy-six people died.

The Grand Jury Rejects Conspiracy Theories

Oklahoma County Grand Jury

In the following report the Oklahoma County Grand Jury summarizes its findings. After an exhaustive study including hearing 117 witnesses and reviewing 1,909 exhibits, the Grand Jury rejected the charge that the federal government had prior knowledge of the attack. It also dismissed the theory that there was a Middle Eastern terrorist connection to the blast, as well as the assertion that there was a connection with a white supremacist organization. The Grand Jury also, after studying many ballistic reports and listening to expert witnesses, rejected the claim that there was more than one bomb set off. Finally, they agreed with the FBI finding that there was no as yet unidentified John Doe No. 2 involved in the bombing.

W e, the Grand Jury, duly empanelled on the 30th day of June, 1997, and charged with the responsibility of investigating all public

SOURCE. "Final Report of the Grand Jury, Oklahoma County," oklahomacounty.org, December 30, 1998. www.oklahomacounty.org.

offenses against the State committed or triable within Oklahoma County as contained in the petition for calling of the Grand Jury duly filed in the Office of the Court Clerk of Oklahoma County on June 2, 1997, and having in a fair and impartial manner, to the best of our abilities and understanding and with due regard to the Court's instructions, and having heard 117 witnesses and received 1,909 exhibits and having fully considered any and all complaints alleged to exist in Oklahoma County, and having been in session for 133 working days, and having heretofore after due deliberation voted according to law, the Grand Jury submits to this Honorable Court its Final Report. . . .

> The so-called Middle Eastern connection . . . based on the evidence available, we believe simply did not exist.

We shall now try to address some of the various allegations presented to us by some of the petitioners.

Allegations Concerning John Doe No. 2

Approximately 26 witnesses testified to the Grand Jury they saw John Doe II or saw Timothy McVeigh with John Doe II. Often the testimony of these witnesses conflicted with each other and these sightings were reported after composites were shown on television or after Timothy McVeigh was led from the Noble County Jail on April 21, 1995.

Based on the descriptions of these witnesses John Doe II would have to be as follows: Height: 5'3" to 6'3"; Weight: 140 pounds to 210 pounds; Build: slim and skinny to stocky and muscular; Race: white, Hispanic, Middle Eastern or Asian; Skin color: white, olive or dark; Hair color: dark blond, red, brown or black; Hair length: crew cut, 2 inches long or shoulder length; Facial hair: mustache or none.

We believe that the most likely identity of John Doe II was that of Todd Bunting, who with Michael Hertig

Photo on following page: The rear axle of the bomb-carrying truck used in the Oklahoma City bombing was a key piece of evidence in the trial of Timothy McVeigh. The car the axle struck was more than 500 feet away from the truck. (AP Photo/Justice Department.)

was in Elliott's Body Shop on April 18, 1995. The similarity of Mr. Hertig to the composite of John Doe I and the similarity of Todd Bunting to the composite of John Doe II are remarkable, particularly when you take into account Mr. Bunting's tattoo of a Playboy bunny on his upper left arm and the fact he was wearing a black T-shirt and a Carolina Panthers ball cap when he was at Elliott's Body Shop.

Some of the other claims regarding John Doe II were:

1. The so-called Middle Eastern connection which, based on the evidence available, we believe simply did not exist.

2. The FBI expended over a million man-hours and spent millions of dollars tracking John Doe II and Middle Eastern connection leads and interviewing the people who called in the reports. All came to nothing. The most promising lead, involving a man named Robert Jacks, or Jacques, also dwindled away as the FBI pursued it.

3. After the bombing an APB was issued for a brown pick-up truck which was reported speeding away from the vicinity of the Alfred P. Murrah Federal Building. Shortly before 9:00 A.M. on April 19, 1995, an employee of the Journal Record Building received a call that one of her children had become ill at school. She got in her brown pick-up, matching the description given on the APB, and left the Journal Record parking lot at a high rate of speed.

4. It would seem that everybody who saw a Ryder truck on April 19, 1995, saw Timothy McVeigh in it. Some of the sightings had the effect of canceling each other out as Timothy McVeigh could not have possibly, or physically, been at such widespread locations, at the same time.

However, in spite of all the evidence before us we cannot finally put closure to the question of the existence of a John Doe II. We are encouraged that the FBI continues to have an agent assigned full-time to the Alfred P. Murrah Federal Building bombing and are confident that if any new evidence comes to light, they and other law enforcement agencies will pursue those leads.

> "An allegation surfaced that agents of the Bureau of Alcohol, Tobacco and Firearms (ATF) assigned to the Oklahoma City Office were contacted on their pagers on the morning of April 19, 1995, prior to 9:02 a.m. and were advised not to come into the office."

The Federal Government Did Not Have Prior Knowledge?

1. Part of this Grand Jury's responsibility was to investigate allegations that federal government agencies had received prior warning the bombing of the Alfred P. Murrah Federal Building was to occur. More specifically, an allegation surfaced that agents of the Bureau of Alcohol, Tobacco and Firearms (ATF) assigned to the Oklahoma City Office were contacted on their pagers on the morning of April 19, 1995, prior to 9:02 A.M. and were advised not to come into the office.

   Four employees of the ATF who were in the building prior to 9:00 A.M. on April 19, 1995, appeared before us and testified. Additionally, we have received photographic evidence and the testimony of other witnesses. We are convinced that ATF employees Luke Franey, Valerie Rowden, Vernon Buster, James Staggs and Alex McCauley were in the building when it was destroyed. There was no credible evidence presented to us that leads us to believe the ATF had prior warning of the bombing.

2. In January, 1998, for the first time, another allegation relating to prior knowledge surfaced. This

allegation focused on a claimed comment by a local United States Congressman the night of the bombing. We heard the testimony of the people who claimed to have heard the comment, the Congressman, and the person who was supposedly with the Congressman that night. We have concluded that whatever words were said (and there was a dispute about this between those who claimed to have heard and those who supposedly said something) they were not evidence of prior knowledge by the Congressman.

No Link Between McVeigh and White Supremacists

After the bombing of the Murrah Building allegations surfaced that an individual identified as an informant for the ATF had provided information to the ATF prior to April 19, 1995, that the Alfred P. Murrah Federal Building was going to be bombed.

> We have made every effort to try to identify any plausible connection between [white supremacists] and the bombing . . . [and] have been unable to find such a connection.

The allegations were basically that several "white supremacists" with connections to Elohim City, a small white separatist community located in Sequoyah County, Oklahoma, may have been involved in the bombing. We have made every effort to try to identify any plausible connection between these individuals and the bombing. In spite of a possible telephone call from Timothy McVeigh to Elohim City in April, 1995, we have been unable to find such a connection. It is our understanding that the FBI has also been unable to find such a link.

No Evidence of a Government "Sting"

There were rumors of a government "sting operation" that went wrong. Knowledgeable witnesses testified under oath and with full knowledge of the law pertaining to perjury, that this was simply not so. We agree. Our view is that everything else in this regard is either fabrication or uninformed speculation.

Allegations of Suspicious Phone Calls

We investigated several telephone calls that have been called suspicious by some people. These calls and our findings regarding them follow.

1. Fire Chief Charles Gaines received a telephone call allegedly from "Gilmore with OSBI" on April 14, 1995, with a warning to be aware of something that may happen on April 15, 1995. The caller was not specific. It was not unusual to receive such calls. Chief Gaines passed the call on to Dispatch with instructions to notify the chiefs and safety officers. As an Oklahoma City Fire Department District Chief, Harvey Weathers was quoted regarding this call in *USA Today*.

   Additionally, Jon Hansen, Assistant Fire Chief, was paged and made aware of the telephone call taken by Gaines and understood that they needed to be aware of a possible Seron Gas incident similar to Japan. He made an attempt after the bombing to find out who.

2. Opal's Answering Service took calls for the U.S. Secret Service in the Alfred P. Murrah Federal Building, one of their 600 clients. Opal's Answering Service has been answering their calls since 1974, and on Saturday, April 15, 1995, at 7:45 A.M., they took a call in regard to a possible terrorist attempt. The operator asked if this was an emergency and the answer was no. The caller said "it's a hunch, I've been up all night thinking about it." On Monday, April 17, 1995, at 8:38 A.M. the call was relayed to the Secret Service. We received into evidence a typed record of the call and determined the call was not specific and this call was not unusual. The

Opal's employee who took the call remembered it right after the bombing and reported it to her supervisor who in turn called the Secret Service.

3. Among the many rumors brought before the Grand Jury was a report of a telephone call allegedly made to the Department of Justice in Washington, D.C., stating the caller was across the street from the Murrah Building which had just been blown up. This call was supposedly made thirty-eight minutes prior to the actual bombing.

The Justice Department employee who took the call later worked out the timing of the telephone call he had received from Oklahoma City. He was able to determine the time based on a package delivery. The actual time was determined to be after the bombing.

> Another strange call was reportedly made to the Respiratory Research Unit of Walter Reed Army Institute of Research, Washington, D.C. The call was made on Monday, April 17, 1995, by a person who identified himself as being a Pentagon Congressional Liaison Officer representing the Governor of Oklahoma.

4. Another strange call was reportedly made to the Respiratory Research Unit of Walter Reed Army Institute of Research, Washington, D.C. The call was made on Monday, April 17, 1995, by a person who identified himself as being a Pentagon Congressional Liaison Officer representing the Governor of Oklahoma. The caller was inquiring about how to treat victims of a blast and what type of medical team and equipment would be required to treat such victims. None of the persons involved could recall the caller giving his name. None of them could recall any specific reference to a bombing in Oklahoma City. We were unable to find the source of this call.

5. We also learned of a telephone call made from a pay telephone at a Taco Bell on April 12, 1995, at

4:00 P.M. to 911. The call was taken by an Oklahoma City Police Department dispatcher, and she recalls it was a bomb related call and was categorized as a signal 8, meaning a mentally ill person. We received an audio tape of the telephone call. Police officers responded to the Taco Bell and talked to the individual who made the call. His address was a home that cares for the mentally disabled. The dispatcher, with 20 years experience, felt the caller knew about a bombing that was to occur, but had no specifics and never mentioned a Federal Building. We listened to a tape of the call and there was nothing specific mentioned.

> The dispatcher, with 20 years experience, felt the caller knew about a bombing that was to occur, but had no specifics and never mentioned a Federal Building. We listened to a tape of the call and there was nothing specific mentioned.

6. The FBI emergency headquarters in Oklahoma City had 25 operational communication lines provided by Southwestern Bell. One of which was previously assigned to a R.D. Hardin. This communication line was added to the Command Post billing on April 19, 1995. This would explain a telephone call made from Hardin's previous number on the 27th of April to the [prosecution witness and co-conspirator Michael] Fortier's in Kingman, Arizona. This call was verified by Agent Jon Hersley and by Southwestern Bell's billing records.

No Unusual Explosives in the Murrah Building

We investigated claims that explosives were found in the Alfred P. Murrah Federal Building. Our investigation determined as follows:

1. A desk ornament that looked like a bundle of dynamite with a clock attached to it. The desk ornament belonged to an ATF agent, and was not an explosive device.

2. Several federal law enforcement agencies were housed in the Alfred P. Murrah Federal Building. Small arms and small arms ammunition were not an uncommon discovery throughout the search and rescue phase.

3. An inert T.O.W. missile was found and mistaken for a secondary explosive device. The inert T.O.W. missile belonged to the U.S. Customs Department.

4. Based on our review of video tapes and photographs, packages of small arms ammunition were mistaken for packs of C4 explosive by one Oklahoma City Police Department officer.

Quick Response Does Not Mean Prior Knowledge

Our investigation revealed:

1. Many who heard the blast and could see the smoke knew something was wrong.

2. The following departments dispatched themselves and did not wait for a call:

   Fire station No. 1 at 820 N.W. 5th

   Fire station No. 4 at 100 S.W. 4th

   Fire station No. 5 at N.W. 22nd and Broadway

   Fire station No. 6 at 620 N.E. 8th

3. A Prayer Breakfast for law enforcement being held at the Myriad in downtown Oklahoma City was adjourning at the time of the explosion.

4. Oklahoma Highway Patrol Bomb Squad was conducting a previously scheduled training session at

36th and Martin Luther King Boulevard in Oklahoma City.

5. Oklahoma City Police Department is located at 701 Colcord, about four blocks away from the Alfred P. Murrah Federal Building.

6. Oklahoma County Sheriff's Department is located at 201 N. Shartel, less than five blocks away from the Alfred P. Murrah Federal Building.

7. Oklahoma City Police Department had officers on patrol in downtown Oklahoma City.

8. Oklahoma County Sheriff's bomb truck was at the Oklahoma County Sheriff's Office Training Center, N.E. 36th and Air Depot, at the time of the blast and responded immediately.

> " There is absolutely no support that [the] prompt response [from first responders to the blast] was evidence of prior knowledge and we do not understand why others have tried to twist this into something evil. "

We conclude that these responding units, as well as many other law enforcement officers, medical personnel and other citizens who responded to the building so promptly should be congratulated. There is absolutely no support that this prompt response was evidence of prior knowledge and we do not understand why others have tried to twist this into something evil. . . .

Only One Bomb Was Used

Based on our investigation we believe that there was a single bomb.

1. Testimony about sound waves and layers of the earth's crust, and that ground waves travel faster than air waves rendered the two-bomb theory inconclusive. The seismograph closest to the Alfred

P. Murrah Federal Building recorded one blast. The seismograph in Norman recorded two sound waves. This was explained due to the density of the earth's crust. The first was the ground wave followed by the airwave five seconds later. The farther the waves go the more separation in time the waves get until they can no longer be measured.

2. The burns on the victims and the building from the blast depict a definite pattern of a singular explosion according to the expert testimony. The intensity and the direction of the burns and debris substantiate only one bomb. The greater distance from the detonation site less debris was found. The rebar in the building was bent in many directions because of falling debris. . . .

Media Coverage Affected Reports of Ryder Trucks

Many people say they saw the Ryder truck at Geary Lake. The problem with this is that they say they saw the Ryder truck at Geary Lake at times and dates which conflict with other sightings. The Ryder truck we believe to be carrying the bomb was picked up on Monday, April 17, 1995.

Many sightings placed a Ryder truck at Geary Lake before the 17th. Some reported that the Ryder truck was seen with the Mercury Marquis. Many describe a Ryder truck with cabover and others with no side door at Geary Lake.

Only two witnesses came forward and talked to the FBI about seeing a Ryder truck at Geary Lake before the stories about the lake were aired in the media. One witness said he saw a Ryder truck with a dark colored pick-up truck parked next to it at around 7:45–8:00 A.M. on April 18, 1995. The other witness described the Ryder truck as having a Bronco type vehicle or dark pick-up parked next to it at 9:00 A.M. on the same day.

On May 2, 1995, the FBI set up a road block to find out whether other witnesses had seen the Ryder truck. It was there that all kinds of Ryder truck sightings were reported. Witnesses described a Ryder truck with trailer, a cabover Ryder truck, or a 15 foot Ryder truck. Numerous witnesses did not report seeing a Ryder truck at Geary Lake until after media coverage.

After the bombing on April 19, 1995, the FBI conducted over 35,000 personal interviews worldwide. The Grand Jury has also interviewed numerous witnesses generated by local sources not contacted by the FBI. An on-going investigation is still being conducted by the FBI.

Over 2,700,000 motel records were examined concerning the travels of Timothy McVeigh and Terry Nichols prior to the bombing. These were achieved by canvassing the areas around the telephone calls attributed to the Daryl Bridges [an alias used by McVeigh and Nichols] phone card. Timothy McVeigh had registered at ten different motels and Terry Nichols had registered at four.

There were 685 calls on the Daryl Bridges phone card between November 1993 and April 17, 1995. 101 pay telephones were used along with eight residential listings. There were no more calls made on the phone card after Timothy McVeigh's arrest on April 19, 1995. Timothy McVeigh, Terry Nichols, and Marife Nichols were the only names established on the Daryl Bridges phone card.

The FBI's intense investigation consisted of over two million man hours along with tens of thousands of other man hours from local authorities.

The FBI set up a 1-800 communication line immediately after the bombing. Anyone who thought they had any information could call the FBI at absolutely no expense. This line is still in active service and is being monitored by the FBI, who take the information and investigate any leads to a logical conclusion.

For the first 10 days (April 1, 1995, through April 29, 1995) the communication bill for the FBI's emergency command post alone was $18,540.02. . . .

The Grand Jury's Final Conclusions

This Grand Jury is convinced that most witnesses who came before us described events that they believed to be true and accurate accounts of what they had observed. In some cases, their testimony could not be substantiated by any other evidence we could find.

There was unfortunately another group of witnesses who testified before us on issues that were not relevant or were found to be nothing more than a recitation of the already numerous and varied cover-up and conspiracy theories.

During the course of this Grand Jury's investigation, we have observed a tremendous amount of journalistic overlap in a number of magazines, books, talk radio shows and Internet websites. The same misprinted information is repeated over and over again without anyone validating its veracity. Sadly, these organizations and individuals have glorified those convicted in federal court by vilifying the federal government and increasing the public's distrust of its government by providing half-truths, uncorroborated, and oftentimes out-right false information.

We would like to specifically address each of the falsehoods asserted by these individuals. Unfortunately, due to the current status of the law in the State of Oklahoma, we cannot specifically mention individual's testimony or comment on the motivation or professionalism of certain other individuals. We can and have, however, expressed our appreciation towards those individuals that are worthy of such.

We are aware that no matter what we do we will be criticized by some. We rely on the common sense of the public to recognize the motives for such criticism. As 14 individuals that have met for 18 months, we brought to this Grand Jury a wealth of diversity. We dedicated ourselves to trying to find out the truth. In spite of those who criticized us and our legal advisors, we worked hard and we were not distracted. We persevered and continued to focus on our task.

> " We also do not believe that this was a sting operation that went too far or that this was a terrorist attack financed or conceived by individuals outside of this country. "

After meeting 133 days, hearing 117 witnesses, listening to over a hundred hours of video and audio tapes, and thoroughly examining several thousand pages of exhibits, we can state with assurance that we do not believe that the federal government had prior knowledge that this horrible terrorist attack was going to happen. We also do not believe that this was a sting operation that went too far or that this was a terrorist attack financed or conceived by individuals outside of this country. This was an act perpetrated by Americans on Americans. Our First Amendment provides for the freedom of speech. Seizing upon this Constitutional right, certain individuals have published and personally profited off books illustrating recipes for such destruction. This was an act that could have been carried out by one individual. We cannot affirmatively state that absolutely no one else was involved in the bombing of the Alfred P. Murrah Federal Building. However, we have not been presented with or uncovered information sufficient to indict any additional conspirators.

As Americans we do not want to believe that fellow Americans could plot, scheme and carry out such a cowardly act in the name of protest. Tragically this is the current reality of the world in which we live. City, county, state and federal law enforcement agencies should be praised for the manner in which they handled this tragedy on the scene, and additionally for the manner in which they investigated and quickly apprehended those responsible.

A Journalist Connects the Oklahoma City Bombing to Other Terrorist Attacks

William F. Jasper

The author of the following viewpoint asserts that Ramzi Yousef, the instigator of the 1993 World Trade Center bombing and Timothy McVeigh, the Oklahoma City bomber, are connected through Terry Nichols, McVeigh's co-conspirator. Nichols made trips to the Philippines in the early 1990s, according to the writer, and was associated with several Middle Eastern terrorist elements, including Yousef. He also made telephone calls to untraceable numbers in the Philippines. He also contends that McVeigh was seen in the company of a Middle Eastern man on the day of the bombing, and asserts that his investigations show that the bombing was a Middle Eastern terrorist plot. President Bill Clinton and Attorney General Janet Reno, however, blamed Oklahoma City

SOURCE. William F. Jasper, "Terror Trail: WTC, OKC, 9-11," *New American*, vol. 18, no. 13, July 1, 2002, pp. 18–23.

on the radical right-wing antigovernment movement for political reasons, he claims. William F. Jasper joined the John Birch Society staff in 1976, and is the senior editor of the *New American* magazine, a self-described right-wing publication.

Ramzi Yousef, the reputed mastermind of the 1993 World Trade Center bombing, sits in a federal maximum-security prison in Florence, Colorado, serving a life sentence. Terry Nichols, the convicted co-conspirator of Timothy McVeigh in the Oklahoma City [OKC] bombing, is incarcerated in the Oklahoma County Jail. He faces a life sentence without parole for the deaths of eight federal law enforcement agents in that 1995 bombing, as well as an upcoming state trial for the deaths of the 161 men, women, children, and unborn baby not named in the federal indictment. Osama bin Laden, the alleged instigator of the September 11th holocaust, is on the run (if alive) with a $25 million bounty on his head.[1]

> Journalists and congressional investigators are beginning to connect the dots and trace the terror trail backward from [the] 9-11 attack to Oklahoma City and the earlier World Trade Center bombing.

This terrorist trio has more in common than shared infamy; evidence indicating that they are actual co-conspirators in a global terrorist network continues to mount. At long last, journalists and congressional investigators are beginning to connect the dots and trace the terror trail backward from last year's 9-11 attack to Oklahoma City and the earlier World Trade Center bombing. . . . Some even suggest that 9-11 might have been prevented if officials had fully investigated the Oklahoma City bombing conspiracy.

Even the Establishment press is coming close to breaking out of its self-imposed muzzle on this subject.

The lead story in the major broadcast and print media for June 4th [2002] announced that Khalid Shaikh Mohammed, already one of the FBI's 22 "Most Wanted" for earlier terrorist acts, is now also being sought by U.S. intelligence and law enforcement officials as a key operative in the Black Tuesday attacks on the World Trade Center and the Pentagon. A federal jury has charged Mohammed, a 37-year-old Kuwaiti, for collaborating with Yousef on both the 1993 World Trade Center bombing and a failed 1995 terror plot to bomb multiple airliners in a single day, or, as an alternative, to hijack and crash airliners into famous U.S. buildings. Both Yousef and Mohammed have long-established ties to Osama bin Laden's al-Qaeda terrorist organization.

Following the Trails of Evidence

According to the *New York Times'* James Risen, a detailed financial investigation of the money trail from the 9-11 plot over the past few months has led officials to believe that Mohammed played a far more prominent role than they had earlier suspected. The developing evidence, said Risen, "could also help explain why Al Qaeda decided to attack the trade center again, to try to finish the job that Mr. Yousef started nearly nine years earlier."

The growing media acknowledgment that the 1993 and 2001 World Trade Center (WTC) attacks are directly connected is a major development; the same trail of evidence will lead honest inquirers to realize that the OKC bombing and other major attacks are also part of an ongoing, coordinated terror offensive. All of which is immensely pertinent to the current hot debate over who knew what and when they knew it, concerning our incredible 9-11 intelligence failures. Answering these questions is essential not only for establishing accountability for these deadly failures, but, more importantly, for averting future terrorist events. They are crucial to fixing the policies allowing the terrorist networks to enjoy easy access to, and operational freedom within, the United States.

Yousef, Nichols, and bin Laden in the Philippines

The trails of Yousef, Nichols, and bin Laden converge in the Philippines as early as 1991. Bin Laden and his brother-in-law, Mohammed Khalifa, set up al-Qaeda operations in the Philippines in the early 1990s, working closely with the terrorist Abu Sayyaf Group.

Intelligence experts believe Yousef, an Iraqi, is an operative for Saddam Hussein's intelligence service. Yousef and his co-conspirators are not "Islamic fundamentalists"; they were known for being very secular: drinking alcohol, partying, frequenting night clubs, "shacking up" with women, and using profanity. Dr. Laurie Mylroie, perhaps the leading authority on Yousef, writes in her book, *The War Against America*, that "Yousef is definitely not a radical Muslim. . . . If Yousef ever spent any time [fighting] in Afghanistan, he would have been in Najibullah's [Communist] camp rather than with the Islamic mujahedin."

According to the signed statement of confessed Abu Sayyaf terrorist Edwin Angeles, he met in Davao City on the Philippine island of Mindanao in 1991 with Nichols, Yousef and other co-conspirators in the 1993 WTC bombing. Angeles, aka Ibrahim Yakub, a co-founder and second-in-command of the Abu Sayyaf Group, said in his handwritten statement:

> I certify that Terry Nichols was known to me personally during our meeting with Abdul Hakim Murad, Wali-Khan and Ahmed Youssef [Ramzi Yousef] in [unintelligible] Davao City on Nov. 1991; Aim to establish a group and organize a Muslim and non-Muslim youth for a cause; we will also to [sic] plan for following: bombing activities; providing firearms and ammo; training in bomb making and handling. . . .

Smoke billows from the World Trade Center's twin towers after they were struck by planes hijacked by terrorists. Many conspiracy theories connect the attack on September 11, 2001, to the bombing in Oklahoma City. (**Ezra Shaw**/Getty Images.)

The Bojinka Plot

Abdul Hakim Murad and Wali-Khan Amin Shah were convicted along with Yousef on September 5, 1996, in the so-called Bojinka Plot, and presently reside in American prisons. Bojinka (Serbo-Croatian for "loud bang") was Yousef's code name for his terror scheme to blow up 11

U.S. jetliners in a single day. A variation of the plan called for crashing or "dive-bombing" planes into U.S. buildings, as Yousef's al-Qaeda comrades did last September 11th. The plot was foiled when the Manila apartment Yousef and Murad shared caught on fire from chemical bomb components they were mixing. Murad was captured in the Philippines following the apartment fire, but Yousef escaped, as he did following the 1993 WTC bombing. With cooperation from Murad and Shah, Yousef was later tracked down and captured in Pakistan, where he was hiding in a guest house rented by a bin Laden company.

Murad's statements to Philippine police and to U.S. officials have been largely ignored, but have huge significance for the OKC and 9-11 attacks, as well as potential future attacks. Important information in Murad's file statements include:

Suicide hijackings. A January 20, 1995, Philippines police report tells of the Yousef/Murad plot presaging the 9-11 attack, in which Murad said he had planned to "hijack said aircraft, control its cockpit and dive it at the CIA headquarters. There will be no bomb or any explosive that he will use in its execution. It is simply a suicidal mission that he is very much willing to execute." Another hijacker was to fly a second plane into the Pentagon or the World Trade Center.

Hijacker pilot training. Murad detailed his pilot training instruction at several flight academies in the United States. The importance of this could not have been lost on federal authorities. In 2001, in the months preceding the 9-11 attacks, U.S. prosecutors focused on al-Qaeda use of U.S. flight schools in their high-profile trial of four men charged in the 1998 bombings of U.S. embassies in Kenya and Tanzania. Essam al-Ridi, an Egyptian trained at a Texas flight school, was one of their star witnesses. Ihab Ali Nawawi, identified by prosecutors as a member of Egyptian Islamic Jihad and a bin Laden confederate, had received pilot training at the same school in Norman, Oklahoma, near Oklahoma City, where some of al-Qaeda's 9-11 hijackers were trained.

Shoe bombs. The world was introduced to shoe explosives when passengers aboard American Airlines Flight 63 from Paris to Miami on December 22, 2001, subdued Richard Reid, a British al-Qaeda recruit, while he was attempting to ignite his shoe bomb. Abdul Hakim Murad's Philippine police report for March 4, 1995, notes that Yousef "taught Murad how to smuggle chemicals and explosive devices inside the airport passing through several [of the] airport's security arrangements," and that Yousef would hide detonators and timing devices inside his shoes. Yousef used these methods on December 11, 1994, to smuggle a bomb on board Philippines Airline Flight 434. On this practice run for the multiple-flight Bojinka plan, the bomb detonated, killing a Japanese passenger, but did not destroy the jetliner.

The Philippine police officials most closely involved in the Bojinka investigation have expressed shock at the failure of U.S. officials to apply the lessons of that case. "It's so chilling," says Senior Inspector Aida D. Fariscal, the policewoman who uncovered the plot at Yousef's smoking apartment. "Those kamikaze pilots trained in America, just like Murad." "The FBI knew all about Yousef's plans," she said, in an interview with former *Wall Street Journal* reporter Matthew Brzezinski for the *Toronto Star*. "They'd seen the files, been inside 603 [the apartment bomb factory]. The CIA had access to everything, too. . . . This should have never, ever been allowed to happen. All those poor people dead."

General Avelino "Sonny" Razon, one of the lead investigators in the Bojinka case, was so shocked at what he saw on September 11th, reported Brzezinski, "that he jumped on a plane in Cebu, where he was now police chief, and flew to Manila to convene a hasty press conference." Razon stated that there was simply "too much coincidence" between 9-11 and Bojinka, particularly since the attacks had occurred within one week of the anniversary of Yousef's conviction for the Bojinka plot on September 5, 1996.

"We told the Americans about the plans to turn planes into flying bombs as far back as 1995," Razon complained to reporters. "Why didn't they pay attention?"

There was much, much more that U.S. officials had not paid attention to. On April 19, 1995, Abdul Hakim Murad sat in jail in New York awaiting trial on the Bojinka plot when news of the Oklahoma City bombing reached him via radio. Murad reportedly told prison guard Lt. Philip Rojas that the bombing was the work of the "Liberation Army." Sufficiently concerned about this statement, prison officials notified the FBI, which sent two agents to investigate. The standard FBI report on the incident, known as a "302," states that "Murad responded to the guard's question by stating that the Liberation Army was responsible for the bombing." The FBI 302 then notes: "A short time later, Murad passed a note to the guard, again claiming that the Liberation Army was responsible for the bombing in Oklahoma City."

> Considerable circumstantial evidence exists linking [Terry] Nichols to [a Middle Eastern terrorist] plot.

According to Edwin Angeles—who, remember, was leader of the Abu Sayyaf Group in the Philippines and a co-conspirator with Yousef, Nichols, Murad and Shah— the "Liberation Army" Murad referred to was the Palestine Liberation Army, working with Islamic Jihad. And according to the U.S. Justice Department, Islamic Jihad and al-Qaeda have virtually merged into one group. Adding to the significance of all this is Oklahoma bombing co-defendant Terry Nichols' role.

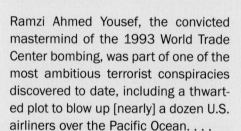

Ramzi Ahmed Yousef's Oklahoma City Connections

Ramzi Ahmed Yousef, the convicted mastermind of the 1993 World Trade Center bombing, was part of one of the most ambitious terrorist conspiracies discovered to date, including a thwarted plot to blow up [nearly] a dozen U.S. airliners over the Pacific Ocean. . . .

Project Bojinka was Yousef's most elaborate and ambitious scheme . . . to date. He planned to blow up 11 U.S. airliners, almost simultaneously, over the Pacific Ocean, using small but strategically placed bombs made of liquid nitroglycerin, which could pass through airport detectors unnoticed and could be assembled in an airplane bathroom using little more than two batteries and a watch.

While planning Project Bojinka, Yousef also hatched a plan to assassinate Pope John Paul II. During this time, he may also have taken part in yet another ambitious conspiracy. Sources, most notably Timothy McVeigh's trial lawyer, Stephen Jones, believe Yousef consulted with Terry Lynn Nichols, one of the men convicted in the Oklahoma City bombing. In November 1994, Nichols flew to the Philippines for an extended stay. A former member of [Filipino terrorist organization] Abu Sayyaf turned informant claimed that a man called "the farmer," who may or may not have been Nichols, met with Yousef and two of his Project Bojinka associates, [Abdul Hakim] Murad and Wali Khan Amid Shah, to discuss bomb making and other terrorist activities. . . .

Yousef was flown back to the United States quickly after his arrest to await trial for the 1993 World Trade Center bombing and the Bojinka plot. On September 5, 1996, Yousef, Murad, and Shah were all convicted for the bombing and assassination conspiracy. Yousef was also found guilty of the bombing of [Philippine Airlines] Flight 434 and the death of Haruki Ikegami, the passenger who died in the bombing. In November 1997, he was also found guilty of the World Trade Center bombing.

SOURCE. *"Yousef, Ramzi Ahmed (1968–),"* Encyclopedia of Terrorism, *vol. 1, Harvey W. Kushner, ed. Thousand Oaks, CA: Sage Reference, 2003, pp. 415–417.*

Terry Nichols's Role

In addition to the testimony of Edwin Angeles, considerable circumstantial evidence exists linking Nichols to the Bojinka plot. There is even more evidence tying the Oklahoma City bombing to Middle Eastern terrorist elements. Consider:

- Nichols made many trips to the Philippines, sometimes staying for weeks or months, without any known means of support. Some of these trips coincided with the period during which Yousef was operating out of the Philippines. Moreover, the areas in which Nichols chose to stay were remarkable for an American because they were areas of the Philippines known for strong Islamic activism and Abu Sayyaf activity.

- Nichols renounced his U.S. citizenship and married a Filipina whose family was known to have connections to Abu Sayyaf.

- Nichols' Filipino father-in-law, Eduardo Torres, stated that he had seen a book in Nichols' luggage on how to build bombs.

- The Justice Department's star witness in the OKC bombing trial, Michael Fortier, testified that a few months before the Oklahoma bombing Nichols had been unable to detonate even a small milk carton of ANFO [ammonium nitrate-fuel oil]. Yet Nichols and McVeigh were credited with constructing and detonating an ANFO bomb, not only bigger than anything ever previously set off in the U.S. by terrorists, but one also nearly 100 percent efficient in burning all of its explosive components. A more likely explanation is that they had help from experts like Yousef.

- Nichols made many unexplained telephone calls to the Philippines, including some to untraceable numbers. This would seem to fit Yousef's modus operandi of using rental cellular phones to avoid surveillance.

- Nichols was in the Philippines when the apartment fire foiled the Bojinka plot. Like Yousef, he fled, breaking the excursion ticket he had purchased earlier and booking a one-way ticket back to the United States.

- U.S. federal undercover informant Cary Gagan has stated that Nichols was present at a meeting in Henderson, Nevada, involving Iranian or other Middle Eastern individuals, where some of the plans for the OKC bombing were made. . . .

The Middle Eastern Connection

In the immediate aftermath of the April 19, 1995, bombing of the Alfred P. Murrah Building in Oklahoma City, *The New American* began reporting on the extensive eyewitness testimony and law enforcement documentation concerning the involvement of Middle Eastern individuals. Regular readers of *The New American* will recall that shortly after the explosion an "all points bulletin" [APB] went out over the Oklahoma City Police radio band. The APB told law enforcement officers to be on the lookout for a "late model, almost new, Chevrolet, full-size pickup. It will be brown in color with tinted windows, smoke-colored bug deflector on the front of the pickup." The APB also stated that the vehicle was occupied by "Two Mideastern males, 25 to 28 years of age, six feet tall, athletic build, dark hair and a beard." . . .

In its 11-count indictment handed down on August 10, 1995, the federal grand jury in Oklahoma City charged that Timothy McVeigh and Terry Nichols "did knowingly, intentionally, willfully and maliciously conspire, combine and agree together and with others unknown to the Grand Jury to use a weapon of mass destruction . . . resulting in death, grievous bodily injury and the destruction of the building." A multitude of credible witnesses had reported seeing Timothy McVeigh on the morning of the bombing or in the days immediately before it with individuals other than Terry Nichols. Some of those witnesses described the individuals as appearing to be of Middle Eastern or Arabic ethnicity.

One individual identified by witnesses as a suspect seen fleeing from the immediate vicinity of the Murrah building right after the blast was Hussain al-Hussaini, a former Iraqi soldier who had entered the U.S. after the Persian Gulf War as a refugee. Al-Hussaini was the subject of a series of investigative reports on the OKC bombing by KFOR-TV, the NBC affiliate in Oklahoma City. We do not know if al-Hussaini, or other former Iraqi soldiers with whom he associates, were involved in the bombing, but, as we have reported previously, strong evidence supports that conclusion. It is obvious that additional accomplices assisted McVeigh and Nichols. The extensive evidence reviewed and uncovered during our seven-year investigation of the bombing points to the involvement of a network of Middle Eastern terrorist cells. President [Bill] Clinton and Attorney General Janet Reno, however, were determined to pin the blame on their political opposition, the "anti-government" forces of the "radical right." They went to extreme lengths to twist, cover up, and destroy any evidence and exclude all witnesses that might contradict this thesis. The OKC bombing terrorists they allowed to escape very likely played a role in the even more monstrous 9-11 attacks.

> The extensive evidence reviewed and uncovered during our seven-year investigation of the bombing points to the involvement of a network of Middle Eastern terrorist cells.

Note

1. Osama bin Laden was killed by US special forces on May 2, 2011.

Timothy McVeigh Insists John Doe No. 2 Does Not Exist

Kim Cobb and Michael Hedges

In the following article, the *Houston Chronicle* reports on a letter written to them by Timothy McVeigh in which he categorically denies the existence of John Doe No. 2, despite claims to the contrary by his defense attorney, Stephen Jones. In his letter, according to Cobb and Hedges, McVeigh asserts that if a John Doe No. 2 did exist, Jones would probably not still be alive. Cobb and Hedges also report that co-conspirator Terry Nichols's defense team argues that John Doe No. 2 was McVeigh's co-conspirator, not their client Nichols. Federal prosecutors, on the other hand, argue that John Doe No. 2 was simply a case of witness mistake, and that such a person never existed. The authors conclude that McVeigh's letter and admission of guilt would make it highly unlikely that he

SOURCE. Kim Cobb and Michael Hedges, "John Doe No 2 Doesn't Exist, McVeigh Maintains in a Letter," *Houston Chronicle*, May 15, 2001. Copyright © 2001 by Houston Chronicle Publishing Company. Reproduced with permission of Houston Chronicle Publishing Company in the format Other book, CD ROM, DVD ROM via Copyright Clearance Center. All rights reserved.

would be granted a new trial. Kim Cobb and Michael Hedges were staff writers at the *Houston Chronicle* at the time this viewpoint was written.

W ith his execution on hold and his attorneys re-viewing old leads about possible accomplices, Timothy McVeigh has written a letter to the *Houston Chronicle* stating unequivocally that there was never a "John Doe No. 2."

Legal experts say the statement, in McVeigh's own distinctive handwriting, could weaken any argument his attorneys might make to seek a new trial based on the possible existence of other conspirators in the 1995 bombing of the Alfred P. Murrah Building in Oklahoma City, in which 168 people were killed and hundreds injured.

McVeigh dated his single-page letter May 2 [2001]—a full week before the FBI revealed it had found 3,135 documents about the bombing investigation that it never shared with the defense. Many are "tips" that reportedly did not pan out from people who claimed to have seen a man with McVeigh in the days before the bombing. The suspect came to be known as "John Doe No. 2."

McVeigh's letter came in response to a reporter's in-quiries about renewed allegations by his estranged trial attorney, Stephen Jones, that McVeigh has always in-flated his role in the bombing to serve his ego.

Jones claims McVeigh was ac-tually the tool of a larger group of conspirators.

"Jones has been thoroughly dis-credited, so I'm not going to break a sweat refuting his outlandish claims point-by-point," McVeigh wrote. "The truth is on my side."

> Timothy McVeigh has written a letter to the *Houston Chronicle* stating unequivocally that there was never a "John Doe No. 2."

Jones says the attorney-client privilege no longer exists between himself and McVeigh, based on the condemned man's widely published confessions to the bombing and on McVeigh's claims that Jones misrepresented him. McVeigh clearly disputes that, noting in the letter that Jones' "ethical transgressions" will have to be judged by his peers and the courts.

"And last, does anyone honestly believe that if there was a John Doe #2 (there is not), that Stephen Jones would still be alive? . . . Think about it," McVeigh wrote.

McVeigh, 33, had been scheduled to die Wednesday for the bombing. But after learning of the existence of the unreleased FBI documents, U.S. Attorney General John Ashcroft delayed the execution for one month, to June 11.

Robert Nigh of Tulsa, one of McVeigh's current attorneys, told CNN's *Late Edition Sunday* that his client might rethink his previous decision to abandon all appeals and seek execution in light of the revelations the FBI had withheld evidence against him.

But on Monday, Nigh said he could not comment on McVeigh's statement to the *Chronicle*, mailed from a federal prison in Terre Haute, Ind., or on whether it would hamper any attempt to seek a new trial based on the newly revealed evidence.

McVeigh's Letter Hampers Attorneys

"Well, it certainly doesn't help," said Robert Pugsley, a constitutional law expert at Southwestern University School of Law in Los Angeles.

If the theory is that newly revealed FBI documents might contain leads to other people involved with McVeigh as accomplices, McVeigh's own words are at odds with the position his attorneys might take, Pugsley said.

If he were McVeigh's attorney, Pugsley said, he'd be upset by the communique. McVeigh has, in effect, ambushed his own attorneys with this statement, he said.

US attorney general John Ashcroft announced on May 11, 2001, that the execution of Timothy McVeigh would be delayed because FBI investigation documents were withheld from the defense. (**Manny Ceneta/AFP/Getty Images.**)

"Well, I bet he wishes now he'd followed my advice and kept his mouth shut," Jones said. "And I bet he wishes he'd followed (appellate attorney) Nathan Chambers' advice and not dismissed those appeals."

Jones said the defense team pursued the trail of John Doe No. 2 aggressively, adding, "Our defense at trial was the John Doe No. 2 was killed in the explosion."

But McVeigh took another swipe at Jones' pursuit of other conspirators by including a copy of a letter written to him in prison by a woman (whose surname is Smiley) who asked, "Was Elvis involved in the bombing?"

McVeigh attached a pre-pasted note to the woman's odd letter and wrote: "Jones and Smiley, kindred spirits."

"I never entered this to be a popularity case, so if Tim doesn't like me, I'm sorry," Jones said. "I was right (that) the government was withholding things, and I was right (that) Tim should have kept his mouth shut. But not everybody has the strength to admit they've made a mistake, even when their life is at issue," Jones said.

Unlike McVeigh, convicted co-defendant Terry Nichols has always embraced the possible existence of "John Doe No. 2" and is asking the U.S. Supreme Court to consider whether the revelation of the FBI documents could cast doubt on Nichols' guilt. The high court recently let stand lower court decisions denying Nichols a new trial.

John Doe No. 2 Was the Result of Witness Mistake

The FBI eventually determined and prosecutors argued that the mystery man sketched in a nationally distributed FBI flier was a case of witness mistake.

> 'To a defense lawyer, John Doe No. 2 materials are a fertile source of exculpatory . . . material.'

"At trial (prosecutors) contended that John Doe No. 2 did not exist and had the significance of 'Elvis sightings,' whereas Mr. Nichols argued that John Doe No. 2 does exist and that he, not Mr. Nichols, was Mr. McVeigh's accomplice," Nichols' attorneys argued in their latest appeal to the Supreme Court.

Nichols attorney Susan Foreman wrote, "To a defense lawyer, John Doe No. 2 materials are a fertile source of exculpatory . . . material. In a case of this magnitude, where the defendant's life and liberty were at jeopardy . . . it is essential the defense have every opportunity to review and assess the withheld materials."

Nichols was convicted of involuntary manslaughter and conspiracy in the bombing. He was sentenced by

U.S. District Judge Richard Matsch to life in prison but still faces state murder charges in Oklahoma that could lead to a death sentence.

The Supreme Court has rarely granted a request for a rehearing once an appeal has been denied. But while legal experts say McVeigh's previous admissions of guilt likely would scotch any attempts at a new trial, Nichols has always claimed innocence and his jury was unable to reach a verdict on sentencing.

FBI and Justice officials have insisted that the documents, which came to light during a months-long project to archive all materials related to the case, were withheld by mistake and that they would not have altered the result of McVeigh's trial or sentencing.

Ashcroft, who ordered the Justice Department's office of inspector general to investigate the FBI's failure to release all documents, has put a high priority on that review, a Justice Department official said Monday. That review has already begun, the official said.

An Investigator Claims to Have Found John Doe No. 2 and Links to 9/11

Doug Hagmann

In the following essay, a private investigator reports on a homeless man, Hussain al-Hussaini, arrested in Quincy, Massachusetts, in March 2011. He claims that al-Hussaini is a person of interest in the Oklahoma City bombing case; that the FBI lost affidavits identifying al-Hussaini as John Doe No. 2 and refuses to release security camera footage of Timothy McVeigh in the company of al-Hussaini; and that al-Hussaini was connected to the attacks of September 11, 2011. He concludes that the FBI's handling of the Oklahoma City bombing case was "terribly wrong" and that the cover-up continues "at the highest level of government." Doug Hagmann is the founder and director of the Northeast Intelligence Network, a private investigative agency that investigates potential terrorists and maintains a website to increase public awareness.

SOURCE. Doug Hagmann, "'Homeless' Man Hussain Hashem al-Hussaini is 'John Doe #2' in Oklahoma Bombing," *Canada Free Press*, March 11, 2011. http://canadafreepress.com. Copyright © Douglas J. Hagmann, Northeast Intelligence Network. All rights reserved. Reproduced by permission.

On Wednesday [March 9, 2011], a "homeless man" was arrested in the Boston suburb of Quincy, Massachusetts, on a charge of assault and battery with a dangerous weapon after allegedly striking another man with a beer bottle. His name is Hussain Hashem al-Hussaini, although [he] has several other aliases and a previous arrest record.

His arrest would have likely gone unnoticed except for the tenacious investigative journalism conducted in the months and years following the 1995 bombing of the Murrah Federal Building in Oklahoma City by author and investigative journalist Jayna Davis. Ms. Davis, a former reporter for KFOR-TV at the time of the bombing, identified al-Hussaini as the "John Doe #2" in the April 19, 1995, bombing that claimed the lives of 168 people, including 22 children, three who were unborn. Her investigation is chronicled in her book, *The Third Terrorist*, and is an important investigative report into the actual events that took place in the months, days and weeks leading to the bombing, and perhaps even more importantly, in the years afterward.

> The disheveled homeless man arrested . . . is at the epicenter of . . . inexcusable failures . . . of the FBI that led directly to the events of September 2001.

The disheveled homeless man arrested this week is at the epicenter of a plot that involves not only domestic terrorism, but the inexcusable failures and activities of the FBI that led directly to the events of September 2001. Ms. Davis documented the direct involvement of a Muslim terrorist operation involved in the 1995 bombing, and attempted to warn the FBI of additional attacks being planned. Despite impeccable documentation compiled by Ms. Davis that I personally reviewed in my capacity as an investigator, her warnings went unheeded. Six years later, the worst attack on American soil killed another 3,000 people. It is my belief that the attacks of

9/11 could have been stopped had the FBI acted upon the evidence she submitted to the FBI.

Affidavits Place al-Hussaini at the Oklahoma Bombing

Instead, twenty-two witness affidavits she compiled and submitted to the FBI in January 1999 that, in part, connect al-Hussaini to the events of the bombing "disappeared." Those affidavits contain sworn statements of multiple witnesses who placed al-Hussaini in the company of Timothy McVeigh prior to the bombing, exiting the Ryder truck that was used for the bombing, and speeding away from the area just prior to the blast. Despite solid witness statements, the FBI reportedly failed to interview al-Hussaini.

In addition to the "hands-off" approach with al-Hussaini, the FBI continues to refuse the release of closed circuit camera footage that exists of McVeigh and "John Doe #2" as they exited the Ryder truck in front of the Murrah Building. Why?

Leading up to, and at the time of, the Oklahoma City bombing, Hussain al-Hussaini worked for a property management company owned by a Middle Eastern businessman who was suspected of having ties to the Palestinian Liberation Organization (PLO). Six months prior to the bombing, this man hired several former Iraqi soldiers. Four years earlier, he had been convicted of federal insurance fraud.

In mid-May 2005, I personally conducted an on-site investigation of "John Doe #2" in Boston. My confidential 30-page investigative report was submitted to the U.S. Department of Justice on 1 June 2005. The information contained in that report verified all of the relevant aspects of Ms. Davis' claims as they pertained to

> Hussain al-Hussaini . . . has been identified [as] . . . accompanying Timothy McVeigh in the Ryder truck . . . [and] stepping out of the Ryder truck at ground zero minutes before the blast.

Hashem al-Hussaini. The following is a redacted version of my partial investigative findings from 2005.

An Investigation of al-Hussaini

The primary subject of this investigation is Hussain al-Hussaini, an Iraqi national who has been identified in sworn witness statements obtained by Ms. Davis as, in part:

1. Accompanying Timothy McVeigh in the Ryder truck used to deliver the bomb to the Murrah Federal Building on 19 April 1995;

2. Stepping out of the Ryder truck at ground zero minutes before the blast;

3. Speeding away from downtown Oklahoma City immediately after the detonation of the truck bomb;

4. Being seen in the company of Timothy McVeigh at various times and locations prior to 19 April 1995.

Hussain al-Hussaini, a former member of the Iraqi military and Saddam [Hussein]'s elite Republican Guard, currently resides in Braintree, (Norfolk County) Massachusetts, a southern suburb of Boston. As well documented in *The Third Terrorist* by Jayna Davis, al-Hussaini came to the U.S. following the Persian Gulf war in 1991 under the guise of escaping persecution from the Iraqi dictator. Because of the significant number of refugees admitted into the U.S. and other factors, the checks-and-balances that were (or should have been) in place to verify the authenticity of those seeking entry into this country were admittedly strained or not properly implemented. Regardless of the reason, al-Hussaini remains living in the U.S. as of the date of this report.

> Subsequent to the Oklahoma City bombing, al-Hussaini . . . worked at Boston Logan International Airport . . . during the time leading up to and including September 11, 2001.

Subsequent to the Oklahoma City bombing, al-Hussaini moved to Dallas, Texas, and then to Boston, Massachusetts, where he worked at Boston Logan International Airport. At that time, he resided with two Iraqi men (brothers) who provided food catering services for the commercial airlines at Boston Logan during the time leading up to and including September 11, 2001.

The two Iraqi brothers referenced above have been identified as Khalid and Majed. They both continue to reside in Braintree, Massachusetts. Due to their close proximity to the primary subject and their activities in Oklahoma City near the time of the 1995 bombing, this investigator has also conducted comprehensive database research and an on-site investigation and covert surveillance to update their activities as well.

Both men were observed at their residence. The activities of both men were documented, and their activities undocumented by law enforcement, according to a source contacted within the FBI. According to this source, they have "no interest" in either subject.

Al-Hussaini's Multiple Identities

Investigation determined that Hussain al-Hussaini possesses a social security number issued in 1994 in the state of Massachusetts. For reasons unclear, it was reissued in Texas in 1995. Several dates of birth are associated with al-Hussaini, all listing his month and year of birth as September 1965. He also has a lengthy list of aliases, including but not limited to Hussain Hashem Jassem Al-Hussaini, Hussain Hashem Al-Hussaini, Hanan Hashim Jassem Al-Hussaini, Adnan Hashim Jassem Al-Hussaini, Salem Hashim Al-Hussaini and eleven others.

Neighbors as well as fellow employees knew him simply as "Sammy."

At the time of this investigation, al-Hussaini was working as a landscaper while living with his 30-year-

old American girlfriend, her father, and a two-and-a-half-year-old daughter. He has resided at this location since 1997. Distinctive in his appearance, he has [a] tattoo reflective of his association with the Iraqi National Guard.

Also at the time of this investigation, the two Iraqi brothers who provided food catering services at Boston Logan on 9/11 were investigated. The reports of their activities, although redacted here, were detailed in my 2005 report submitted to the U.S. Department of Justice. Yet, much like the warnings of Ms. Davis, nothing has taken place.

Massachusetts State Police troopers armed with automatic weapons patrol the terminal at Boston's Logan International Airport on September 15, 2001. Some assert that Hussain al-Hussaini was "John Doe No. 2," and that he worked at Logan airport on 9/11. **(AP Photo/ Michael Dwyer.)**

Al-Hussaini Predicted Tragedy

Confidential psychiatric records confirm that in 1997, Hussain al-Hussaini made a foreboding prediction about a future event to take place at Boston Logan International Airport, the point of origin for two of the four hijacked flights that slammed into the World Trade Center on September 11, 2001.

According to those records and prior to 9/11, al-Hussaini suffered anxiety so acute regarding his airport job at Boston Logan International that he checked into a psychiatric hospital to seek treatment for recurring panic attacks. When asked about the source of his trepidation, he told his therapist "if something happens there, I will be a suspect."

Interestingly, only days after my investigation into the activities of Hussain al-Hussaini, he "disappeared." He left his residence of eight years and slipped quietly into the shadows of Boston, only to be found homeless and facing criminal charges this week.

Something is terribly wrong with the FBI's handling of the 1995 bombing and the events leading up to and including the attacks of September 11, 2001. Something at the highest levels of government that continues through the present.

The Media Misrepresented the Militia Movement's Involvement in the Oklahoma City Bombing

Mack Tanner

The following viewpoint argues that the national media unfairly smeared the entire militia movement after the Oklahoma City bombing due to Terry Nichols's (Timothy McVeigh's co-conspirator) association with the Michigan Militia. The author asserts that the media painted militia organizations as groups of radical, right-wing extremists bent on the destruction of the federal government. He refutes this portraiture through an investigation of the movement, interviewing many militia members across the country. What emerges from the investigation, he says, is a picture of solid citizens who not only fear the federal government, but who are also

---

SOURCE. Mack Tanner, "Extreme Prejudice: How the Media Misrepresents the Militia Movement," *Reason*, vol. 27, no. 3, July, 1995, pp. 42–50. Copyright © Reason Foundation. All rights reserved. Reproduced by permission.

training to defend themselves against the government's abuse of power. Mack Tanner is an Idaho-based writer who formerly spent twenty-five years in the US diplomatic service. He is a frequent contributor to *Reason*, a self-described libertarian magazine.

"Who could possibly have done such an evil, cruel act?"

It's a question that we all asked ourselves as we watched the TV images of a demolished building filled suddenly with the dead, the dying, and the terrorized.

For a day, reporters and terrorism experts told us the bombers were almost certainly Muslim terrorists from the Middle East. Then the FBI captured a suspect who turned out to be one of our own—not just an American, but one who had served in our military and fought in one of our wars. Shocked that an American could do such a thing, reporters went looking for a bigger story.

The Media Casts the Militia as a Threat

The FBI wasn't about to throw the case by talking details. But the news media needed scary people to show to a public ravenous for answers. So the media told us that the FBI's primary suspect, Timothy McVeigh, and his two alleged co-conspirators, Terry and James Nichols, had some kind of association with something called the Michigan Militia. Then they gave us hours of TV coverage on what they repeatedly described as an extreme right-wing, anti-government, armed-and-dangerous group of paranoid Americans.

> The media told us with lots of film clips . . . that the militia movement represents a threat to American society every bit as serious as Middle Eastern terrorists.

Never mind that leaders of two different militia groups in Michigan insisted that the suspects were not members of any militia group, and that indeed, they had been ejected from a meeting because of their extreme and violent talk. The media told us with lots of film clips of Americans training in the woods that the militia movement represents a threat to American society every bit as serious as Middle Eastern terrorists.

Reporters had seemingly reliable sources to back their conclusions. Last October [1994], the Anti-Defamation League and the Southern Poverty Law Center's *Klanwatch* had issued separate reports warning of the "danger posed by the growing white supremacist involvement in newly formed citizen militias." Both groups had urged Attorney General Janet Reno "to alert all federal law enforcement authorities to the growing danger posed by the unauthorized militias," several of which had allegedly been infiltrated by white racists and anti-Semites.

The national media responded to the two reports with alarm-bell-ringing accounts of the troubling militia movement. These groups, according to press accounts, were preparing for armed clashes with their own government. And even when reporters didn't accuse the militias of violent racism, they described them as "a right-wing counter-culture" of "fearsomely aggressive adherents" engaged in the "politics of paranoia," to quote a *Los Angeles Times* account. Television exposés ran film clips of men and women dressed in combat fatigue uniforms, carrying military style semi-automatic weapons as they trained for combat.

Understanding the Militia Movement

I had learned about the militia movement several months before the Oklahoma tragedy while cruising the Internet newsgroup talk.politics.guns. The messages posted there by computer literates explaining and defending the militia movement didn't read like the ravings of white racist paranoids looking for an excuse to go to war with the government. They described the militia movement as a reasonable extension of the philosophy of armed self-defense. If one keeps weapons to protect one's family against the criminal intruder, doesn't it also make sense to prepare for the possibility that the government may turn criminally violent? There are plenty of 20th-century precedents for fearing that might happen in our country, as it has in others.

Of course, such arguments sound rational only to someone who believes that the Second Amendment confirms an individual's unalienable right to own and bear firearms—to someone who believes that an armed citizenry, like a free press, is an important bulwark of liberty. These arguments assume that the Framers of the Constitution intended that armed citizens would serve as the ultimate check on government power. Militia supporters argue that arms are most valuable as deterrents, whether to prowlers or out-of-control government agents.

Hoping to understand the militia movement, I sent a few of my own messages over the Internet. Working from the initial e-mail contacts, I interviewed citizen militia leaders, members, and people friendly to the militia movement in Texas, Michigan, Ohio, South Carolina, Montana, Wisconsin, California, Washington, and my own home state, Idaho. What I learned about the movement suggests that its motivations, members, attitudes, and tactics have been grossly mischaracterized by culturally ignorant reporters more concerned with telling sensational stories than with explaining the more-complicated truth. . . .

A Typical Militia Member

"One thing we definitely are not are haters of government or haters of law enforcement," Bob Clarke, a member of the Michigan Militia told me a few days after the Oklahoma tragedy. "I have a driver's license, license plates, and I pay my taxes." Like many militia members, Clarke is a devout Christian who educates his children at

The Michigan Militia Defines "Militia"

The militia is: all able-bodied citizens who are capable of bearing arms; the absolute last line of defense against any threat to the State or Country, whether that threat is natural or man made, foreign or domestic.

Our motivation is patriotism and a sincere desire to defend the Constitution. Our goal is to encourage all citizens to achieve a high level of preparedness for a wide variety of possible emergencies.

We support a Constitutionally limited government and defend the American ideals of Life, Liberty and the pursuit of Happiness. We are open to all citizens regardless of race, sex, religion, or political affiliation. Groups not open to public membership and/or which are organized for any other purposes are not militias. The militia, as an organization, has no religious theme; is not racial in nature; nor does it advocate terrorism or violence.

SOURCE. *Michigan Militia, "In Defense of Liberty II," www. michiganmilitia.com.*

home. He sees his participation in the militia movement as a continuing part of the Christian life. His reaction to the Oklahoma bombing is no different from any other American's: "Let's get them, find out who did it. Whoever did it is despicable. Any human being has to be appalled."

Clarke, who owns a computer service company, is a fairly typical militia member in both his background and motivations. Contrary to what some left-leaning analysts have claimed, militia members aren't drawn primarily from the ranks of the unemployed and economically disenfranchised. Like Clarke, they are solidly middle class. And, like Clarke, they are driven not by hatred—of blacks, Jews, or even the government—but by fear. They worry that the federal government does not respect the liberties guaranteed in the Constitution and may eventually pose a direct threat to them, their families, and their neighbors.

Although they have a host of popular grievances with the federal government—from land-use policies to gun control to just about everything the Department of Education does—militia members are clearly [worried] most about armed federal attacks. Most of the groups were organized sometime after the events at Ruby Ridge, Idaho, where, in 1992, U.S. Marshals and FBI agents killed Randy Weaver's son and wife, and the deadly 1993 standoff between the feds and Branch Davidians at Waco, Texas. . . .

> [Militia members] believe that maintaining freedom depends, ultimately, on the deterrent of an armed populace.

Like ACLU [American Civil Liberties Union] lawyers who rely on the courts or intellectuals and journalists who rely on the press, militia members have a theory of how best to protect American liberties. They believe that maintaining freedom depends, ultimately, on the deterrent of an armed populace.

Nonetheless, says the [unidentified Michigan Militia] training officer, "We don't wear our camo all of the time. We are not looking for an armed confrontation if we can avoid it. Every week, we pick a political issue based on what the media is reporting, and we crank out a letter on that issue which each member sends to his congressman or senator." Militia members are fond of saying that Americans' freedom rests on five boxes: the soapbox, the ballot box, the jury box, the witness box, and the cartridge box. . . .

Media Ignorance

It's [the] suggestion of armed defense that troubles critics. Sane, civilized Americans aren't supposed to mention the possibility that their government could turn violent—and certainly aren't supposed to suggest that they might take up arms against it in self-defense.

When Richard Cohen, writing about the militia movement in the *Washington Post*, states that "they are armed to stay armed, a tautology that apparently is the sum and substance of their ideology," he demonstrates his ignorance of the political and social culture of those who join the militias. People don't join a militia because they love guns, but because they believe that guns are necessary tools if they are to keep all the other freedoms they enjoy.

Cohen suggests that the Second Amendment "is an 18th century anachronism, incompatible with 20th and 21st century America." But militia members are looking at a 20th-century example in which a democracy devolved in less than a decade into a tyranny that first outlawed private ownership of firearms, then marched 6 million law-abiding people, beginning with its own citizens, to their death. Contrary to the portrait of them as raving anti-Semites, militia members are haunted by the same example that frightens their detractors at the Anti-Defamation League. . . .

Militia Members Defend Themselves

[Many] militia units are open to the public and don't exclude anyone. But they can discourage racist talk. Says Sheryl Tuttle, a movement supporter who lives in southern Idaho, "I remember once when somebody did make a racist remark in one of our meetings. Someone else got up immediately to call him on it. He never came back to another meeting."

Tuttle and her husband Bill are typical militia supporters. In their mid-40s, they've raised one child and are now grandparents. Sheryl is active in her church's work with

Michigan Militia leader Normon Olson swears in new recruits on December 11, 1994. Olson and other militia group leaders deny any link between their organizations and the Oklahoma City bombing. **(Michael Samojeden/AFP/Getty Images.)**

children and has served as an informal foster mother for several kids. She left a career in nursing several years ago to work with Bill designing and producing welded metal art pieces, which they sell at craft shows. When she started traveling between shows with sizable sums of money, Sheryl bought a semi-automatic pistol and started carrying it. Twice since then, she and Bill have scared off potential criminals by displaying (but not pointing) their weapons. In one case the threat was a prowler at their home, in the other a tailgater on a steep, deserted mountain road.

Bill, a voracious reader partial to conspiracy theories of history, is a military veteran and the son of a professional Army officer. The Tuttles got interested in the militia movement as a result of their growing involvement in politics and their frustration with government regulations that directly affect their lives and businesses. "Every time we go to a preschool board meeting" at the church, says Sheryl, "we've got another regulation we are supposed to obey. Now they want us to put an elevator in the church where we hold the school."

"Our government was founded on the Constitution and the Bill of Rights, and they have thrown our Constitution out," Bill said, explaining why he joined the U.S. Militia Association.

"Now we have to spend time and energy defending ourselves, instead of doing something more constructive," Sheryl told me when I asked her about the media blitz demonizing the militia movement. "It's going to scare a lot of people, and it scares me, but am I going to back off? No! . . .

Critics of the Militia Are Perverse

Many supporters of an all-powerful central government have a political faith, not a political philosophy. They lack the intellectual tools necessary to challenge and debate alternative political theories. Incapable of understanding the reasons for the voters' revolt in the last election,[1] and convinced of the truth of their own faith, they assume that those who have contrary political beliefs must be evil people.

Obviously, in this world view, those who hold guns while espousing an alternative set of political beliefs must be the most evil people of all. By suggesting that such people inspired the Oklahoma bomb blast, those with blind faith in big government expect to discredit and destroy not just the threat they see in the militia members, but also the much more real threat represented by the last election, the Contract with America, and the growing demand by millions of voters for less government, lower taxes, more effective law enforcement, and more choice for the individual. . . .

Using innuendo, guilt by association, and stereotypes to tar people as racist, anti-Semitic, and potentially violent could be considered as much a hate act as the burning of crosses. Such indiscriminate accusations pin targets on people like the Tuttles by identifying them as objects to be attacked with impunity. This, in turn,

> [Militia members'] most dangerous enemy may not be the federal government but the national news media.

creates the distrust that can result in disastrous confrontations between law enforcement officers and legally armed citizens. That's what happened at Waco. Another such disaster could have happened in Roundup, Montana, in early March [1995]. That it didn't suggests that the militias are more peaceful and rational than their critics make out. . . .

The Most Dangerous Enemy

The events that followed the arrest of Timothy McVeigh suggest that the members of citizen-militia associations may have been fearful of the wrong institution. Their most dangerous enemy may not be the federal government but the national news media.

"When the FBI authorities were quoted, they were all very circumspect," says Bob Clarke. "The press very gladly lumped everybody together as a right-wing extremist, racist type of a cult. It's all the same to them. The media hasn't done a very good job of understanding this whole militia thing. There is a lot of misinformation coming off the airwaves."

There is indeed. After days of watching the media coverage on every one of the three major TV networks and reading through reams of news reports and critical editorial comment, I had neither heard nor read a single shred of court-admissible evidence that suggested that any unit of the militia movement was engaged in any conspiracy to overthrow the government or to commit any other crime in support of their political agenda.

Innuendo and scare quotes, largely taken out of context, dominated the reports. Even the advocates of conspiracy theories, such as Mark Koernke, never call for the overthrow of government in their material. While TV news people can play quotes out of context, anyone who watches hours of his militia videos knows that when a battle-ready Mark Koernke talks about defending one's sector, he's talking about a reaction force resisting an invasion, not the beginning of the revolution.

And some reports seemed deliberately misleading. ABC, for instance, showed a headline from *The Resister*, a publication of the self-proclaimed Special Forces Underground that is read by some militia members. It read: "Would You Shoot Fellow Americans?" ABC didn't tell viewers that the article is an exposé of a survey distributed by a Marine to his troops—not a call to arms.

One may not like the militia movement's political agenda, one may find its members' conspiracy theories troubling, and one may be offended by the idea that middle-class men and women are training with deadly weapons because of a fear that the government may someday attack them. But journalists have a responsibility to be accurate and careful, not merely entertaining and provocative. It is a responsibility they have too often shirked in reports on the militias.

As the Oklahoma bombing investigation proceeds, it is possible that the FBI may find evidence that a militia member or a citizen-militia association was involved in some way. If such evidence is discovered, the people I've met in the militia movement will be the first to cheer as the culprits are led away to jail. But until such evidence is presented in court, the national media have done a great injustice to a group of American citizens who spend their spare time practicing to fight a defensive war rather than playing paintball and who wear camouflage and combat boots rather than jogging shorts and running shoes while they get their outdoor exercise.

Note

1. In 1994, a mid-term national election placed Republicans in the majority in the US House of Representatives for the first time since 1954.

The Militia Movement Continues to Propagate Antigovernment Hate

Abraham H. Foxman

The following viewpoint argues that the Oklahoma City bombing brought to national attention the "potentially violent nature" of militia organizations. The author draws connections among the militia movement, Timothy McVeigh, Terry Nichols, and the writings of former neo-Nazi leader William Pierce. He states that since 2000, terrorist attacks from outside the country have distracted public attention away from the homegrown terrorist threat posed by the militia groups. However, the militia movement has enjoyed a resurgence since the election of US president Barack Obama, and the hatred of these groups toward the federal government has grown. He argues that the groups are armed and training for violent conflict with the government and urges law enforcement to be prepared. Foxman is the national director of the Anti-Defamation

League and the author of *The Deadliest Lies: The Israel Lobby and the Myth of Jewish Control.*

Fifteen years ago, on April 19, 1995, Timothy McVeigh exploded a truck bomb in front of the Murrah Federal Building in Oklahoma City. The explosion killed 168 men, women and children, and wounded hundreds more.

The bombing shocked the nation—and was a powerful reminder that homegrown terrorism could be just as brutal and hateful as terrorism spawned on foreign shores.

Prior to the bombing, a few watchdog organizations had issued warnings about the dangerous growth of right-wing extremist groups, including the then-new militia movement. In 1994 the Anti-Defamation League issued a report titled "Armed and Dangerous: Militias Take Aim at the Federal Government," which turned out, unfortunately, to be extremely prescient.

But it took the bombing itself to make most Americans aware of the seriousness of the threat and the potentially violent nature of these groups and their individual members.

McVeigh and his accomplice, Terry Nichols, had an intense hatred of the government stoked by conspiracy theories of government plots to kill the Branch Davidians during their 1993 standoff with the government. Their actions were further inspired by "The Turner Diaries," a fictional blueprint for a white revolution by former neo-Nazi leader William Pierce.

McVeigh and Nichols were hardly alone. From 1995 into the early 2000s, hundreds of anti-government extremists and white supremacists were convicted for a variety of plots, conspiracies and violent acts.

> The militia movement alone has quadrupled in size . . . with more than 200 active anti-government militia groups.

Over the years, though, other serious crises emerged, including the 9/11 terrorist attacks, the wars in Afghanistan and Iraq, the ongoing threat of another attack by Al Qaeda, and a rise in domestic and international Muslim extremism.

The Lessons of Oklahoma City Are Important

The lessons of Oklahoma City, though not forgotten, somehow seemed less urgent in the new millennium.

Those lessons may be more important today than they have been in many years. . . . Motivated by factors ranging from the recession to the election of Barack Obama as president, the extreme right in the United States has undergone a startling resurgence.

Anti-government movements such as the militia and the sovereign citizen movements have increased greatly in size and activity. The militia movement alone has quadrupled in size over the past two years, with more than 200 active anti-government militia groups. White supremacist movements, though not experiencing the same increase in size, have demonstrated greatly increased levels of agitation, including calls for violence.

Over the past year, right-wing extremists made headlines through violent acts and plots, including a fatal shooting at the U.S. Holocaust Memorial Museum in Washington, D.C., the deadly ambush of three police officers in Pittsburgh, and the gunning down of a physician in his own church in Kansas, among others.

A Recent Example of a Dangerous Militia

The arrest of nine members of the anti-government Hutaree Militia, accused of a plot to kill law enforcement officers and their families to create a confrontation with the government that would spark a broader uprising,

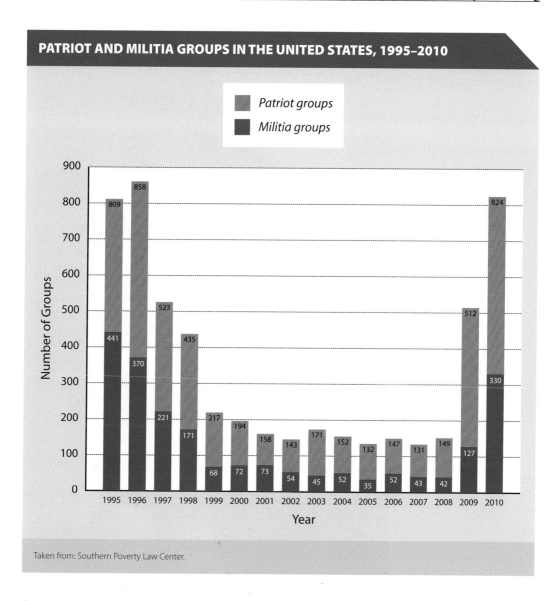

PATRIOT AND MILITIA GROUPS IN THE UNITED STATES, 1995–2010

Patriot groups

Militia groups

Taken from: Southern Poverty Law Center.

was just the most recent example of an extremist militia group making headlines.

For experts who monitor the extreme right, the parallels between today and 1995 are disturbing. Extremists have revived the anti-government conspiracy theories that motivated many plots in the 1990s, ranging from alleged "concentration camps" constructed by the Federal

Law enforcement officers stand outside the US Holocaust Memorial Museum in Washington, D.C., on June 10, 2009, after a security guard was fatally shot by a white supremacist. **(AP Photo/Alex Brandon.)**

Emergency Management Agency to the imminent suspension of the Constitution and imposition of martial law.

Even the Hutaree Militia had ties to militia propagandist Mark "Mark from Michigan" Koernke, the "patriot" leader made infamous during the Oklahoma City investigation after being mistakenly linked to the bombing.

The Growth of the Militia Movement

Militias during the 1990s were largely high profile due to both their presence in the media as well as their increased activity on the Internet. Group websites were dedicated to spreading militia ideologies, posting anti-government propaganda, and recruiting new members. Militias such as the Kentucky State Militia, Michigan Militia, or the Montana Freemen, a Christian patriot group, would often gather for group meetings to discuss conspiracy theories and to receive training in survivalist techniques such as building retreats, self-defense, and learning how to stockpile food and water. Also central to such gatherings was a fascination with weaponry, and members participated in arms training and other para-military activities. It was such behavior that U.S. government and law enforcement agencies feared would encourage many members to engage in more violent and extremist actions directed at government targets.

Militias in the United States have been re-forming and growing in membership since the attacks of September 11, 2001. Some observers have warned of a resurgence of militias in reaction against certain decisions by the current political administration. The Anti-Defamation League has reported that since 2004, various militia groups have had an increase in membership, similar to the increase of militia activity that took place in the early 1990s following the Ruby Ridge and Waco incidents.

SOURCE. *Megan L. Gray and Stephanie Oakley, "Militias,"* Encyclopedia of Race and Crime, *vol. 2. Ed. Helen Taylor Greene and Shaun L. Gabbidon. Thousand Oaks, CA: Sage Publications Inc., 2009, pp. 517–520.*

The anti-government sentiments of the Hutaree Militia are unfortunately shared by a growing number of domestic extremists, both within and outside the militia movement. The Hutaree arrests are important, but there still exist a growing number of extremists who are already armed and preparing for potential conflict with the government.

Monitoring of Internet chatter related to health care reform and other recent issues indicates that many militia members and anti-government extremists believe this legislation will be followed by the mass legalization of illegal immigrants, postponement or elimination of democratic elections, martial law and gun confiscation. Like the Hutaree, they believe that a "New World Order" of tyrannical rule is coming.

Right-Wing Extremism Must Be Monitored

As we remember the victims of the Oklahoma City bombing 15 years ago, and vow that we will never again allow domestic terrorists to strike on our soil, it is essential that our society and law enforcement remains cognizant of the ever-present danger of right-wing extremism in the United States.

Law enforcement agencies should be prepared to apprehend extremists who cross the line from protected speech to illegal actions. Community leaders and elected officials should take this renewed threat of domestic extremism seriously.

The most fitting way to honor the victims of Oklahoma City, and to make sure that their sacrifices were not in vain, is to ensure that no new McVeigh is able to emerge from the shadows to wreak destruction and sorrow.

Timothy McVeigh Deserves the Death Penalty

Paul Baumann

In the following essay, the editor of a national Catholic magazine argues that the Oklahoma City bombing is an "especially heinous crime" and that anyone convicted of the deaths caused by it deserves the death penalty. He states that although Christ teaches that individuals should turn the other cheek when confronted with wrongdoing, the Catholic church does not oppose the death penalty when it is just. Further, he asserts although the death penalty is not a deterrent to crime, justice demands retribution proportionate to the crime, and in some cases this includes execution. Justice must also speak for the victims of the crime, and their voices should not be lost when the court turns its attention to the rights of the criminal. Paul Baumann is the editor of *Commonweal*, a Catholic journal of religion, politics, and culture.

SOURCE. Paul Baumann, "An Editorial Dissent: Death Penalty Favored for Oklahoma City Bomber," *Commonweal*, vol. 122, no. 10, May 19, 1995, pp. 4–6. Copyright © Commonweal. All rights reserved. Reproduced by permission.

Christ's admonition to turn the other cheek has never been written into law, and for good reason. The Sermon on the Mount enunciates a spiritual ideal, not a theory of jurisprudence. The Kingdom of God or the church must not be confused with the political community. Catholicism has traditionally acknowledged the moral legitimacy of the death penalty, just as it has defended just wars, and for similar reasons. In both cases, a defense of the common good justifies the resort to violence.

Those justly convicted for the mass killing in Oklahoma City deserve the death penalty. If justice means anything, it means that the willful, premeditated murder of the innocent cannot be seen to be tolerated. I believe that the execution of Nazi war criminals, for example, was meet and just. The living owe the murdered innocent no less—no less than to assume the full burden of judgment and the responsibility for punishment. The state should end the lives of murderers only for heinous crimes, but it is precisely in those instances that the death penalty alone can express the moral outrage of humanity. Punishment itself expresses and embodies society's moral judgment, and just punishment must fit the crime; it must not be too severe, or too lenient. Unjust punishment or unwarranted leniency undermines our sense of fairness, and thereby the common good. In that sense, the crime of murder is trivialized if we do not reserve the right to inflict the death penalty in the most grievous cases.

Punishment Must Be Proportionate to the Crime

The principal objection to the death penalty is that the state cheapens the value of life if it in turn and in kind becomes an instrument of killing. But the logic of this argument fails to come to terms with the inherently retributive nature of justice in criminal cases. Does holding kidnappers in prison against their will cheapen human

dignity by merely mimicking the crime? That can't be so. Insuring that punishment is proportionate to the crime is the moral dilemma, not the thin paradox of the state resorting to coercion.

Death-penalty abolitionists argue that imposing life terms on murderers leaves the state in a morally superior position. In short, the state avoids getting blood on its hands. I'm not so sure. Convicted killers kill again, either in prison or after they are released. Innocent people are killed as a direct consequence of not imposing the death penalty on the guilty. Those deaths may be a necessary cost of the state washing its hands of direct killing, but it is sentimental to think that outlawing the death penalty will "end the cycle of violence." Neither death-penalty advocates nor opponents can escape with clean hands.

Mickey, Jay, and Shari Sawyer were among the nearly 300 people who witnessed the execution of Timothy McVeigh on closed-circuit television on June 11, 2001. Mickey and Jay's mother, Dolores Stratton, was killed in the bombing. (AP Photo/ Laura Rauch.)

> Justice demands we treat criminals as moral agents responsible for their actions, and that we assume such moral responsibility ourselves.

The church has long accepted the retributive aspect of justice, for without it there can be no individual responsibility and therefore no individual freedom. As [British novelist and philosopher] C.S. Lewis wrote, only a retributive ethic can make the idea of just or unjust punishment coherent. Cures or deterrents either work, or they don't. Justice—moral accountability—involves a different calculus. Justice demands we treat criminals as moral agents responsible for their actions, and that we assume such moral responsibility ourselves. To be sure, retribution must not be just a fancy word for revenge. For that reason, murder is regarded as an assault on the moral order and the community as a whole. Consequently, the judgment rendered by the community through its competent authorities seeks to "redress the disorder caused by the offense," and only indirectly to relieve the agony of individual victims, no matter how grave that private injury may be. It is the deliberations of the law that effect and legitimize the transference of moral outrage from the individual to the community and in so doing help to vindicate the moral order upon which individual rights depend. It is the law that enables us to distinguish justice from revenge and capital punishment from murder. Only in this way has society tamed the righteous anger of victims and prevented individuals from taking the "law" into their own hands.

Still, some argue that only God, no human authority, has the right to take human life, even the life of a justly convicted killer. Traditionally, however, God is understood to be the ultimate source of all authority, not an alternative authority who renders moot the judgments of temporal justice. Indeed, Catholicism has characteristically held that God's authority must be mediated by human institutions. Civil authority is fallible, often woefully so, but it does not follow that we must be agnostic about our ability to seek or render justice in the here and now. Similarly, it cannot be that the more heinous a crime the more futile our judgment becomes, for that would only immunize the most diabolical criminals by virtue of the enormity of their crimes.

Justice for the Dead

An essential element of justice, and one only the community can perform, is to speak for the victims. As [American psychiatrist and bioethicist] Willard Gaylin has written, in our adversarial system the voices and lives of murder victims are quickly forgotten as we direct our attention, necessarily, to the criminal's rights. Once those rights are secured, however, the law surely fails in its primary task—namely, to make human community and life possible—if it does not speak forcefully for the dead

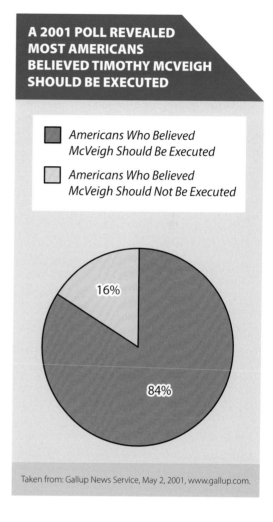

A 2001 POLL REVEALED MOST AMERICANS BELIEVED TIMOTHY MCVEIGH SHOULD BE EXECUTED

■ Americans Who Believed McVeigh Should Be Executed

□ Americans Who Believed McVeigh Should Not Be Executed

16%

84%

Taken from: Gallup News Service, May 2, 2001, www.gallup.com.

and for the moral order of things. That is why the law itself, and the punishment the law demands, does not seek direct compensation for the victims or eventual reconciliation for the criminal, rather it expresses our moral purposes. In punishing, the law articulates and defends the common good. That is why justice must be seen to be done. In imposing the death penalty for especially heinous crimes, the law proclaims in unambiguous terms the value society places on innocent life and the absolute revulsion in which we hold such murders. Moral outrage, mediated by the institutions of justice, is the best way to secure the sanctity of life.

Just as we cannot take the law into our own hands, we cannot replace retributive justice with a disproportionate mercy—and disproportion is what Christian mercy is all about. Finally, only the victims have the right to absolve the killer. Our duty as citizens is to seek justice. That duty is not primarily to ourselves, or to the future, but to the dead.

Timothy McVeigh Should Not Be Executed

Paul Finkelman

In the following viewpoint, a law professor argues that Timothy McVeigh should be imprisoned for life, not executed. He notes that McVeigh was guilty of the crime, expressed no regrets, is not insane, and received a fair trial. However, he explains that there are six arguments against executing him. Keeping him imprisoned for the rest of his life, on the other hand, will allow him to grow old and sick without the fame he so desires; may bring to light the truth about other co-conspirators; and would be a deterrent to other would-be terrorists. Paul Finkelman teaches at the University of Tulsa College of Law.

Timothy McVeigh seems like a poster child for advocates of the death penalty. No one, not even his lawyers, doubts he bombed the Murrah Federal Building in Oklahoma City, killing 168 men, women,

SOURCE. Paul Finkelman, "Why We Shouldn't Execute Timothy McVeigh," *Jurist: The Legal Education Network*, April 23, 2001. Copyright © Paul Finkelman. All rights reserved. Reproduced by permission.

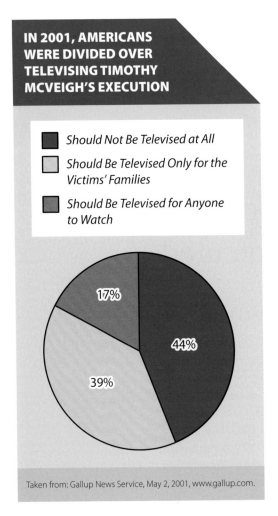

IN 2001, AMERICANS WERE DIVIDED OVER TELEVISING TIMOTHY MCVEIGH'S EXECUTION

■ *Should Not Be Televised at All*

□ *Should Be Televised Only for the Victims' Families*

■ *Should Be Televised for Anyone to Watch*

17%

44%

39%

Taken from: Gallup News Service, May 2, 2001, www.gallup.com.

and children, in the worst single incident of domestic terrorism in the history of the United States. Far from denying his crime, McVeigh is proud of it. He regrets that some children died, but they were, in his twisted mind, collateral damage in his insane war against the United States of America. Clearly, there is no claim of actual innocence here. Unlike so many death penalty cases, we clearly got the right man.

But, if his war was insane, McVeigh certainly was not, at least in a legal sense. He knew what he was doing, meticulously planned it, and fully understood that people would die when his bomb went off. That is what he expected and what he wanted. According to Dr. John Smith, a psychiatrist hired by his own defense team, McVeigh expected to kill upwards of 400 people. Indeed, Smith expressed shock at "the coldness, the almost glee with which he told me the details of the bombing, the expectations that at least 400 people would be killed." In a legal sense, there is no insanity defense here.

Nor can anyone claim McVeigh did not get a fair trial. He had some of the best lawyers in the nation arguing his case. He had the venue changed to a different state. The government provided all the support staff that anyone could ask for.

McVeigh had effective counsel, a fair trial, and a jury correctly found him guilty of a heinous crime. So, how can anyone argue against execution?

Arguments Against McVeigh's Execution

There are in fact six strong arguments against sending McVeigh off to his final reward.

First, there is the traditional ethical argument that the state should never take life when it can avoid doing so. Had McVeigh violently resisted arrest, and died in the process, the state would have taken his life because McVeigh gave society no choice. But, McVeigh does not threaten anyone now, so we need not execute him. Why should society reduce itself to McVeigh's level? His acts are unspeakable—he took the lives of people for no reason, other than to make a statement. Do we do anything different by taking his life?

> In [McVeigh's] mind, he wins by being executed. We win by keeping him in jail for the rest of his life.

Second, McVeigh is certainly not a threat to anyone in the future. He can surely be confined for the rest of his natural life in a one man cell in the bowels of the federal penitentiary in Terre Haute, Indiana. There he can contemplate his crimes, while not ever being able to plant another bomb.

Third, executing McVeigh will fit into McVeigh's game plan. According to a recent book on this killer, McVeigh's final statement will likely contain some version of the words from the poem "Invictus," "I am the master of my fate, I am the captain of my soul." . . . McVeigh stopped all appeals in his case, to speed along the imposition of the death sentence. He is ready to die, and apparently wants to be executed. It is the final act in his drama: he set the stage for his own death, and now is ready to have it carried out. This is reason enough not to execute him. He wants to bring society down to his level, of killing for revenge. In his mind, he wins by being executed. We win by keeping him in jail for the rest of this life.

Fourth, executing McVeigh will also not serve as a deterrent to similar crimes. McVeigh fully expected to

An area outside the federal penitentiary in Terre Haute, Indiana, was reserved for anti-death penalty demonstrators during Timothy McVeigh's execution on June 11, 2001. (Tim Boyle/Getty Images.)

be killed by the police in a shoot-out. He was prepared to die fighting and fully expected to die for his crime. Knowing he might be killed or executed hardly deterred him. And it will not deter anyone else from committing a similar crime. Anyone who is as wicked as McVeigh will not worry about his own life. In fact, executing McVeigh [may] encourage some equally pathetic and evil person to commit a similar crime.

Fifth, executing him prevents us from ever learning the full truth about his co-conspirators. Years from now, after he has been sitting in prison for a long time, he may tell us who else, if anyone, was involved in his plot.

Execution Will Create a Martyr

This leads to the last argument against his execution. Putting McVeigh to death may very well create a martyr. McVeigh knows he is far better off dead than alive. His "cause," such as it is, will be served by his martyrdom. Some other twisted soul, tortured by living in a democracy where there is a general level of freedom and tolerance, will doubtless look on McVeigh as a hero. And, as we all know, a true "hero" must die for his cause. When we kill McVeigh and we complete his plan he becomes the dead "hero," the slaughtered martyr. He gains yet another day, or week, or month of headlines.

But, imagine if we did not kill him? Imagine declaring him "insane," on the very clear theory that no one in his right mind would do what McVeigh did? Reduce his act of terrorism to an act of the irrational, an act of an evil, pathetic mind. Then send him off to live for the rest of his life—another 40 or 50 or 60 years—in Terre Haute. Executed today, he goes to his death young, vibrant, defiant—heroic to the twisted and angry. But, left in his cell, he ages. The "where are they now" pictures show Timmy McVeigh with a cane, wrinkled, raving and angry, frustrated to be alive. Losing his teeth and his hair, rotting away slowly. That would be the appropriate message to the next Timmy the Bomber: that we will not give you the satisfaction of your martyrdom. We will not give the attention you crave and dignify your irrational hatred by even calling it a crime. Instead, we will put you away, where you cannot harm anyone, and leave you there. You will grow old, and sick, and eventually, without fanfare or notice, simply die. Such an inglorious and meaningless ending to the life of Timmy McVeigh, many years from now, would not only be the justice he deserves, but also serve as a deterrent to some would-be mass killer, who would use the death of others as a vehicle for his own fame. It would also send a message that the United States will not lower itself to the level of the Timmy McVeigh's of the world.

CHAPTER 3

Personal Narratives

The Broadcast of McVeigh Audiotapes Causes Unease

Eve Conant

The following viewpoint discusses the release of previously unheard audiotapes of Timothy McVeigh's account of the infamous Oklahoma City bombing. The chilling tapes record McVeigh's lack of regret when he claims that he feels "no shame for it." Although some believe the tapes will offer an insight into the mind of the bomber, some victims believe it will only give further notoriety to a "voice that should remain silent." Eve Conant is a reporter for *Newsweek*.

O n [April 19, 2010], the 15th anniversary of the Oklahoma City bombing, MSNBC's Rachel Maddow will air, for the first time ever, audiotapes of Timothy McVeigh giving his own account of why he detonated a truck filled with explosives in front

Photo on previous page: A woman sits next to her cousin's memorial chair at the Oklahoma City National Memorial. The memorial has 168 chairs, one for each victim. (AP Photo/David J. Phillip.)

of the Alfred P. Murrah Federal Building. It was our country's most destructive and deadly act of terrorism on U.S. soil prior to September 11. The bombing murdered 168 people, including more than two dozen children under the age of 6. More than 800 people were injured; damage was estimated at $652 million. Yet, McVeigh's recorded voice, as if speaking from the grave almost nine years after his execution, says, "I feel no shame for it."

Maddow has said the program is designed to put antigovernment extremism in perspective. "It doesn't have to lead to violence, but it can and it has," says Maddow in promotional spots. "We ignore this, our own very recent history of antigovernment violence and the dangers of domestic terrorism, at our peril." According to the Southern Poverty Law Center, the number of antigovernment extremist groups spiked from 149 in 2008 to 512 (127 of them militias) in 2009.

The tapes will undoubtedly offer insights into the twisted mind of McVeigh. But some victims of his attack, reached by *Newsweek*, say it will grant further notoriety to a voice that should remain silent.

Mixed Feelings over McVeigh's Audiotapes

Dr. Paul Heath, a counseling psychologist in the Veterans Affairs office at the time of the attack and founder of the Oklahoma City Murrah Building Survivors Association, says that the first thing survivors wanted from McVeigh before his death was an apology. "But he didn't say a word. He just looked into the camera and died." The second? "To never hear from him again. And we got that, except for these tapes." Heath helped several survivors exit the building, including one man who was carrying one of his own eyes in his left hand. Heath, who had an encounter with McVeigh days before the bombing, says he will watch the broadcast but doubts other survivors will.

He still has questions for McVeigh, and even gave some to a reporter who interviewed the domestic terrorist years ago. One question: "Why did you flaunt yourself on the Thursday before the bombing? Did you get some sadistic pleasure seeing all of us alive?" When McVeigh came to Heath supposedly looking for work, Heath asked him if he was related to a McVey family that he knew. "McVeigh stuck his long fingers in my face, saying, 'Remember my name is McV-E-I-G-H.' He was delusional." But Heath worked with a lot of people with posttraumatic stress disorder, suspecting McVeigh also suffered from it. "I understand a TV reporter's obligation to share this. I don't have a problem with that. But this won't tell me anything I don't already know."

> 'I find it disturbing that these tapes will be played at such length, giving him—once again—a platform.'

Attorney Beth Wilkinson was the prosecutor who argued for the death penalty for McVeigh. "Obviously I am gratified to know he'll be admitting to what he was convicted of," says Wilkinson. (McVeigh never admitted guilt during his trial or sentencing.) "That said," she adds, "I find it disturbing that these tapes will be played at such length, giving him—once again—a platform." She hopes that the two-hour segment will provide a perspective on extremism, not just McVeigh's. (According to an MSNBC press release, "Survivors and family members of the bombing victims are given a voice in the film, bravely stepping forward to offer the final word on the true impact and meaning of McVeigh's brutal attack.") Before his execution, says Wilkinson, McVeigh agreed to interviews, including *60 Minutes*, on the condition that he not specifically address the crime. "At least now he will be getting press—if that's how to describe it—for what he actually did."

Dennis Purifoy, 58, was a manager in the Social Security office where 16 co-workers and 24 customers were killed, but he was in the safer, east side of the building at the time of the explosion. He helped several people get out of the building, and tried to help workers who were gravely injured and then died. "I'm a Maddow fan and have the utmost respect for her; if anyone can put his actions into context she can," says Purifoy. "But I have mixed feelings about this, mostly negative. In addition to McVeigh being a coward and a liar, you have to remember at the time of those tapes, Terry Nichols was still in the system. In the book, McVeigh went out his way to make him look less culpable." Purifoy says he'll tape the show. "I don't think I've ever really heard his voice. I don't know that I could connect a voice to his face. But the main thing is that that man took his secrets to the grave."

Will Marling, executive director of the National Organization for Victim Assistance (NOVA) says our media obsession with criminals "gives perpetrators prominence; it's the victims who need to be remembered." He says victims can be retraumatized by "trigger events" related to a crime, like anniversaries, court proceedings, parole hearings, and executions. "If the point is education, why not have victims hear the tapes first and then decide if there is educational value? The victims are almost always the last to be consulted." He expects the tapes, like other trigger events, to cause deep upset. "It brings it all up again for the victim. It's heartbreaking to watch a person go right back to that day."

That's why Dianne Dooley probably won't watch on Monday night. Dooley was on the stairwell of the third floor of the Murrah Building when the explosion went off. Bloodied and in shock, she made it to the hospital, her foot damaged, her hand crushed, her arm broken in 12 places. After six surgeries, months of physical therapy and 15 years, she still can't read about McVeigh. Dooley has permanently lost 50 percent of the use of her hand, and gave up her beloved hobby of softball long ago. When he pops up on her TV screen, her stomach churns. "Ugh. I saw a clip about [the MSNBC program] this morning, and I just . . . kind of . . . walked away," she says, laughing a bit nervously. Dooley says there is an awkwardness among survivors, some thinking everyone should move on, others understanding the need to talk. "I don't know that we'll ever understand him, and I don't think hearing from him will prevent someone else from doing the same."

A High School Student Loses Her Father

Miranda Ice

In the following essay, high school student Miranda Ice relates the experience of losing her father in the Oklahoma City bombing. She was at school when she heard about the bombing in her second-hour class. Because her father worked in downtown Oklahoma City, she was worried for his safety. Then her school counselor told her that her father's building had exploded. After returning home, Ice, her sister, and her mother tried to locate her father. They were all relieved when they received word her father was at a local hospital, she writes. However, after a long wait, they discovered it was a man with the same name as her father. For eight days, the family did not know for sure what had happened. Ice's father was found in the wreckage on April 27, 1995.

SOURCE. Miranda Ice, "Sparkling Blue Eyes." Reprinted from *Forever Changed: Remembering Oklahoma City, April 19, 1995*, compiled by Marsha Kight. Amherst, NY: Prometheus Books, 1998, pp. 191–193. Copyright © 1998 by Marsha Kight. All rights reserved. Used with permission of the publisher; www.prometheusbooks.com.

I hated first hour choir at school. Sometimes I would sit there and wish something would happen so I wouldn't have to go for a while. I would never want what happened to my family to happen to anyone else, yet it happened to 167 other families. April 19, 1995, changed my life forever.

Unlike others who heard or felt the bomb, I didn't. I thought it was a normal day. When I got to my second hour, the TV had been turned to the news. The newscasters were talking about a bomb that had blown up the federal building. I began to worry because my dad worked downtown. My best friend, Erin, kept reassuring me that everything was okay. I felt better until my counselor got me out of class to go to her office. I tried to page my dad, but he never returned my call.

News I Did Not Want to Hear

I went back to class and about ten minutes later my counselor came back with news I didn't want to hear. She said that my mom had called and told her it was my dad's building that had exploded. I cannot describe what I felt at that moment. Feelings of total emptiness and numbness consumed my body. I knew things would never be the same again. I felt as though in that short thirty minutes I had aged thirty years.

I went home at lunchtime that day. My mom had called the Red Cross in an effort to find my dad. My sister was already there. She had felt the bomb at her home in Oklahoma City. It seemed like days before the Red Cross called us back. Finally, late that afternoon they notified us that Dad was at St. Anthony's Hospital. I felt so relieved that there was a chance he could be alive. We immediately got in the van and drove to the hospital. When we arrived, we went to a large waiting room with the other families.

> For eight long days we never left the house. It was strange to see the world carrying on when our lives stopped for so long.

Hours of Hope Followed by Cruel Disappointment

There were counselors there and all kinds of food donations. We saw Dad's name on the wall under the list of survivors who had checked into the hospital. All we had to do now was locate him.

After four hours of waiting, we could not understand why they wouldn't tell us where my dad was. I was so mad that I couldn't even speak. I just didn't understand how a hospital could lose a patient. A nurse walked over to my family and told us that Paul Ice had already checked out that afternoon. They also told us that the Paul Ice who had checked out was fifty-seven years old and had a different social security number than my dad. My dad was only forty-two. I couldn't believe there were two Paul Ices! I can remember at that time all the hope I had felt was gone. I knew that I would never see my father's smile again or watch his big blue eyes sparkle. As we stood there in the waiting room, we overheard a nurse talking about someone named Priscilla upstairs in ICU. The only person named Priscilla we knew was Priscilla Salyers, who worked in the office with my dad. My mom and sister asked the nurse if they could go upstairs and talk with her. I stayed in the waiting room for any news of my dad. When they came downstairs, Mom told me it was Priscilla from Dad's office. She told my mom that she and Dad had been talking to each other when the bomb went off. She said the last thing she saw was my dad's blue eyes. And she told my mom she didn't think my dad made it. We waited for a while longer but decided to go home and wait for the Red Cross to call us.

Our Lives Changed Forever

From that day forward we sat in front of the TV and next to the phone. For eight long days we never left the house. It was strange to see the world carrying on when our lives stopped for so long. At 4:30 A.M. on Thursday, April 27,

1995, we got the call we had been expecting and dreading. My dad's funeral was two days later.

In that one moment at 9:02 A.M. on April 19, 1995, our lives changed forever. Not a day goes by that my sister and I don't think about my dad or wonder, What if things were different? I have learned not to dwell on things that never will be. I know my dad would be proud of who Sarah and I have become, and I know he watches over us and cheers us on from Heaven. When I get really depressed or discouraged about something, I close my eyes and in my mind I can see Dad smiling at me, his blue eyes sparkling, giving me his favorite thumbs-up sign!

Revisiting the Oklahoma City Bombing

Andrew Murr

In the following viewpoint, a reporter sets out to collect the oral histories of survivors and witnesses of the Oklahoma City bombing. He describes how six years has not dulled or lessened the pain and tragedy of the bombing. The images and sounds of the tragedy still remain fresh in the survivors' minds, which caused many of them to choke up or even cry when recounting their memories of the Oklahoma City bombing. Andrew Murr is a reporter for Newsweek.

Some remember a deafening roar. Others recall hearing nothing at all. Years later, little Brandon Denny, who barely survived after the bomb blew a large hole in his skull, suddenly turned to his father and asked: "Dad? Do you know what that bomb sounded like?" After being told no, Brandon, now nine, supplied his recollection. "Boom! Shhhhhhhhh," he yelled, pre-

SOURCE. Andrew Murr, "Revisiting the Oklahoma City Bombing," *Newsweek*, June 8, 2001, http://thedailybeast.com. Copyright © 2010 The Newsweek, Inc. All rights reserved. Reproduced by permission.

cisely imitating the blast and the powerful rush of air that followed it.

I cover city hall now, but I've been both police and courthouse reporter. I read autopsies every day on those beats. I flipped through them, glanced at the grim details and tossed them aside in search of a news angle on crime and violence. That's how we survive in this business. We find it, read it and report it.

Six years later, echoes of the Oklahoma City blast still reverberate for survivors, rescuers, investigators and family members of the 168 people killed in and around the Murrah Building on April 19, 1995. This past spring, *Newsweek* decided to collect the oral histories from several of the people who witnessed the tragedy first hand. We wanted to find out how thoroughly people had healed and what sense the victims made of the effects of Timothy McVeigh's act of terrorism.

We approached the task a little nervously. We'd both covered the bombing in 1995 and remembered the oppressive cloud of shock and sorrow that hung over the city. It was a lot easier emotionally to report on the manhunt in Michigan, Kansas or Arizona than face up to the struggles of the survivors and rescuers. We had other worries, too. Perhaps survivors had no desire to relive the past. Maybe they were talked out and didn't want to tell their stories to yet another reporter. But when we finally sat down with them, we had fresh proof that letting people tell a story in their own words brings its own revelations.

Six Years Has Not Dulled the Pain

If we had thought the passage of six years would dull memories or emotions, we were wrong. Images still had the fresh power to horrify. Police detective Don Hull was inside the building in the first hours, pulling survivors and victims out of the rubble. "You'd feel this dripping, like water was dripping on you, but it wasn't water," Hull told us. "You got blood coming from above you, and it's dripping down all over everywhere." John Avera, a former cop, revealed that he spent five years worrying that he may have killed one-year-old Baylee Almon by carrying the child out of the building. Finally last year he was able to see the autopsy that showed the baby was beyond saving. Many participants choked up or cried while recounting their stories.

Survivors and their families were remarkably generous with their time. People who hadn't spoken to reporters in years graciously agreed to open up to us. Most had the conviction that it was necessary to speak and to bear witness. Some coped by remaining very private. Michael Reyes lost his father, Tony, in the blast and could easily have lost his own life as he plunged four floors from his HUD [US Department of Housing and Urban Development] office. A few months ago, he was with a group of new friends when someone brought up McVeigh's impending execution. "I didn't say a word," he told us. "I don't know if the other . . . people knew my connection or not, but it's not something that I was going to point out." Others are compelled to speak out. John Clark was then a police lieutenant but now runs the city's emergency-management unit. He recalls getting angry at an anti-terrorism speaker who avoided mentioning Oklahoma City to spare the feelings of the local listeners. Clark sought him out after the talk. "Buddy, we live with it every day," Clark told the man. "We know what happened. It did happen here."

Both of us were struck by the trauma's lingering effects and the survivors' ability to go on with their lives anyway. Michael Reyes continues to see explosive flashbacks. But he's mastered them. "You just deal with it and go on," he says. Trauma doctor Carl Spengler performed

> 'Buddy, we live with [the bombing] every day. . . . We know what happened. It did happen here.'

Friends, family, and survivors of the Oklahoma City bombing walk through the streets of Oklahoma City during the one-year anniversary remembrance on April 19, 1996. (AP Photo/Brandi Stafford/ Pool/Tulsa World.)

triage on bombing victims in the shadow of the smoking building. Since that day, he's never slept more than four hours a night. But he continues to heal patients. Brandon Denny suffered brain injuries that give him only partial use of his right arm and leg and require speech and occupational therapy to this day. Still, he gamely troops off to school with his sister and fellow survivor Rebecca, happy and content. In their own way, each is making sure that Tim McVeigh's act of terror doesn't dictate their future.

A Young Mother's Dead Infant Becomes an Icon

Aren Almon

In the following essay, Aren Almon recounts the anguish of losing her baby daughter in the Oklahoma City bombing. After dropping her one-year-old daughter, Baylee, off at the day care center in the Murrah Building, Almon, a single mother, went off to work five miles away, where she heard the bomb. When she realized what had happened, she rushed to the site to look for Baylee. She and her family eventually went to a hospital where they learned that her daughter had been killed. The next day, she saw Baylee's picture in the arms of a firefighter on the front page of the newspaper. That photo became the national symbol of the tragedy, appearing on the cover of *Newsweek*. Almon relates that the photo made her recovery from the tragedy significantly more difficult.

SOURCE. Aren Almon, "A Mother's Long Goodbye: One April Morning I took My Daughter to Day Care in Oklahoma City, Minutes Later She Was Dead—The Icon of a Tragedy," *Newsweek*, v. 129, no. 15, April 14, 1997, p. 14. Copyright © Newsweek, Inc. All rights reserved. Reproduced by permission.

Y ou may not realize it, but you know my daughter. She's one of the youngest victims of the Oklahoma City bombing, captured on film as an anguished firefighter held her lifeless body in his arms. That tragic image of her was transmitted around the world the day after the bloody attack. It even ended up on the cover of *Newsweek*; it was an icon of the bombing. But most people don't know how that picture has complicated my own coming to terms with the loss of my daughter, Baylee—one of 19 children who died in the Alfred P. Murrah Federal Building.

As lawyers in the Oklahoma City case select a jury, many victims' families are still wrestling with the tragedy. We are the real people who prosecutors are fighting for. Unlike some, I do not believe the conspiracy theories surrounding this case. Yes, other accomplices may be at large. But I think Tim McVeigh will be found guilty, and that he will pay with the death penalty.

I still live with what happened that terrible morning. On April 19, 1995, I dropped Baylee off at the second-floor day-care center around 7:30 A.M. and went on to work. (I was a single mother.) When the bomb exploded at 9:02, I heard it and felt it at my desk five miles away. Then someone turned on the TV, and I recognized what was left of the Murrah building. My heart sank. I arrived at the building around 9:20. The area was already roped off, and rescuers and bleeding people were everywhere. "What about the babies in the day-care center? What about the children?" I yelled.

> [My daughter was] one of the youngest victims of the Oklahoma City bombing, captured on film as an anguished firefighter held her lifeless body in his arms.

Looking for Baylee

Soon I ran into my parents and sister. They were looking for Baylee, too. We heard that some children had been

Aren Almon, mother of one-year-old victim Baylee Almon, sits by a picture of fireman Chris Fields holding Baylee's lifeless body. (**Steve Liss/Time & Life Pictures/ Getty Images.**)

taken to St. Anthony's Hospital, where Baylee was born. Officials there sent us to Children's Hospital. Children's sent us back to St. Anthony's, where they said a baby remained unidentified. At St. Anthony's I quickly found Baylee's pediatric nurse. "Is Baylee here?" I asked. No, she said; all the surviving children had been claimed. But we heard that a baby remained unidentified? "Oh, my God," cried the nurse. "Let me get Dr. Beavers." (Up to that point I had assumed the unidentified baby was alive.) Dr. Beavers was Baylee's pediatrician. As I sat in the waiting room with my family he rounded the corner. A minister was with him. The unidentified child was Baylee, he said, and she was dead.

We all went down to the hospital's morgue to identify her. As we approached the door I couldn't go in. Daddy went alone. I remember feeling as if the world were passing by. The next morning I asked for the newspaper. My parents had hidden it. When I finally saw a copy, I knew why. There was the picture of the firefighter. "That's Baylee!" I said. Then the swarm started. I was afraid to step in front of my door for fear that someone would take my picture. When the doorbell rang, I froze. One reporter brought Chris Fields, the firefighter in the photo, over to meet me. I told him how glad I was that the rescuers got Baylee out so quickly, and I thanked him for holding her so gently.

> Criticism from other victims hurt, but commercialization of the photo was worse.

Baylee was supposed to be buried on Saturday, April 22. But when Daddy went down to the medical examiner's office, they had misplaced her body. They finally found her, and Baylee was buried on Monday. I had to go out and buy her a burial outfit. That was one of the hardest things I've ever done.

Commercializing the Tragedy

Meanwhile, the photo started bothering some of the other parents who lost children. They began to criticize me in the media for getting too much attention while their children were ignored. I tried to tell them that I didn't want the publicity. But they didn't listen. When the governor suggested that a statue of Chris and Baylee be a memorial, the criticism increased. No one realized that such a memorial would have made my nightmare even worse. Criticism from other victims hurt, but commercialization of the photo was worse. Freelance photographers sold the photo rights, and the picture began showing up on T shirts, lapel pins and even telephone cards. In July of 1995 I ran across one man raffling off eighteen-inch statues of Chris and Baylee. "That's my daughter!" I said angrily. What was his response? He told me to buy a ticket so I could win one. The statues were the last straw. Chris and I filed suit to try to control the commercial use of the photo. A judge has ruled against us, saying I was the only person who could recognize Baylee in the picture. We have appealed.

I'm patching my life together. Therapy has helped a lot. Though I have yet to return to work, last weekend I married Stan Kok, a senior airman at Tinker Air Force Base outside Oklahoma City. I really want to have more children. Before I met Stan, I asked 30 doctors about artificial insemination. They all declined—most said they didn't think I was ready. Stan and I think we're ready now. Three kids sounds about right to us. Things have slowly improved during the last two years [since 1995], but I miss being a mother. I miss being Baylee's mother.

CHRONOLOGY

1968   Timothy McVeigh is born in Lockport, New York, on April 23.

1988   McVeigh joins the US Army and meets Terry Nichols in basic training in Georgia. The two meet up again while stationed at Fort Riley, Kansas, where McVeigh is honored as the top Bradley gunner on the base.

1991   McVeigh begins participation in the Persian Gulf War in January. He is later awarded an Army Commendation Award and a Bronze Star for his performance under fire.

1992   August 21–31: Federal marshals and FBI agents lay siege to survivalist Randy Weaver's home at Ruby Ridge, Idaho, to arrest him on a bench warrant for failure to appear in court. The confrontation ends with the deaths of a deputy marshal, Weaver's fourteen-year-old son, and Weaver's wife.

1993   February 28: The US Bureau of Alcohol, Tobacco and Firearms (ATF) raids the Mt. Carmel compound of a religious cult led by David Koresh, known as the Branch Davidians, near Waco, Texas. Six Branch Davidians and four ATF agents are killed. The raid leads to a standoff that lasts for fifty-one days.

             March: McVeigh, enraged over the situation in Waco, travels to the site, where he distributes antigovernment literature and bumper stickers.

April 19: Federal agents attack the Mt. Carmel compound. In the ensuing fire, seventy-four men, women, and children are burned to death. McVeigh follows the events from Michigan, where he is staying at Terry Nichols's family farm.

May–September: McVeigh follows the gun show circuit, selling guns, antigovernment literature, and survival items. He also reconnects with a buddy from the army, Michael Fortier.

1994: McVeigh moves and takes a job in Kingman, Arizona. He begins building bombs and renounces his US citizenship on March 16.

September: McVeigh plots to blow up the Alfred P. Murrah Federal Building in Oklahoma City.

Fall: McVeigh and Nichols begin stockpiling ammonium nitrate and nitromethane.

December: McVeigh and Fortier drive to Oklahoma City to observe their target.

1995 April 17: McVeigh picks up a rental Ryder truck that he had reserved and made a deposit on days earlier.

April 18: McVeigh and Nichols mix explosives and pack them into the Ryder truck.

April 19: McVeigh lights two bomb fuses shortly before 9:00 A.M., parks the truck in front of the Murrah building, and walks away.
The truck explodes at 9:02 A.M., bringing down most of the building. A frantic search-and-rescue operation begins.

At 10:34 A.M., McVeigh is arrested for driving without license tags in Perry, Oklahoma.

April 21: McVeigh is identified as "John Doe #1" from police drawings. Federal investigators discover that McVeigh is under custody for a vehicle misdemeanor in Perry. He is moved to Tinker Air Force Base and arraigned.

Terry Nichols turns himself in.

April 23: The search for survivors trapped in the wreckage shifts to a body recovery effort.

A memorial service for those who died is held in Oklahoma City with President Bill Clinton and First Lady Hillary Rodham Clinton in attendance.

May 10: Terry Nichols is charged in connection with the bombing of the Murrah Federal Building.

August 8: Michael Fortier and his wife, Lori, testify before a grand jury and agree to cooperate with authorities.

A federal grand jury returns an eleven-count indictment against McVeigh and Nichols.

October: Government prosecutors announce that they will seek the death penalty against McVeigh and Nichols. The US district court judge orders separate trials for the two men.

1996   February 21: McVeigh's and Nichols's trials are moved to Denver, Colorado, because a federal judge rules that they will not receive a fair trial anywhere near Oklahoma City.

1997   April 1: McVeigh's trial begins.

June 3: A federal jury convicts McVeigh on all eleven counts of murder, conspiracy, and using a weapon of mass destruction.

August 15: McVeigh is sentenced to death by lethal injection.

November 4: Nichols's trial begins.

December 24: Nichols is convicted of conspiracy and involuntary manslaughter.

1998   June 5: Nichols is sentenced to life imprisonment.

2001   May 11: McVeigh's execution is delayed until June 11 on the admission of the FBI that they had failed to turn over thousands of pages of documents before the 1997 trial.

June 6: McVeigh's request for a stay of execution is denied, and he instructs his lawyers not to appeal.

June 11: McVeigh is executed at the federal penitentiary in Terre Haute, Indiana.

FOR FURTHER READING

Books

James Bovard, *Lost Rights: The Destruction of American Liberty.* New York: Palgrave, 1995.

Dan T. Carter, *The Road to Oklahoma City: How Some Americans Came to Hate Their National Government.* Atlanta: Emory University, March 1998.

Steven M. Chermak, *Searching for a Demon: The Media Construction of the Militia Movement.* Boston: Northeastern University Press, 2002.

Jayna Davis, *The Third Terrorist: The Middle East Connection to the Oklahoma City Bombing.* Nashville: WND Books, 2004.

Stephen Jones and Peter Israel, *Others Unknown: Timothy McVeigh and the Oklahoma City Bombing Conspiracy.* New York: Public Affairs, 2001.

Douglas Kellner, *Guys and Guns Amok: Domestic Terrorism and School Shootings from Oklahoma City Bombing to the Virginia Tech Massacre.* Boulder: Paradigm Publishers, 2008.

Edward T. Linenthal, *The Unfinished Bombing: Oklahoma City in American Memory.* New York: Oxford University Press, 2003.

Lou Michel and Dan Herbeck, *American Terrorist: Timothy McVeigh and the Oklahoma City Bombing.* New York: Harper Collins, 2001.

Oklahoma Today, *9:02: The Official Record of the Oklahoma City Bombing,* Norman: University of Oklahoma Press, 2005.

Richard A. Serrano, *One of Ours: Timothy McVeigh and the Oklahoma City Bombing.* New York: W.W. Norton & Company, 1998.

Kathleen Treanor and Candy Chand, *Ashley's Garden: Aftermath of Oklahoma City Bombing.* Kansas City, MO: Andrews McNeel Publishing, 2002.

Stuart Wright, *Patriots, Politics, and the Oklahoma City Bombing*. Cambridge: Cambridge University Press, 2007.

Periodicals

Scott Canon, "Oklahoma Jury Takes a New Look; State Legislator's Focus on Conspiracies Prompts Another Inquiry on Blast," *Kansas City Star*, p. A1.

Sharon Cohen and Rex Huppke, "Remorseless to the End; Victims Watch Bomber Die," *Albany Times Union*, June 21, 2001, p. A1.

Todd Copilevitz, "Volunteers Outnumber Survivors; Rescue Response Swift, But Too Late for Many," *Dallas Morning News*, April 20, 1995, p. 27A.

Ambrose Evans-Pritchard, "What Really Happened in the Oklahoma City Bombing?" *Human Events*, vol. 53, no. 41, October 31, 1997, pp. 12–14.

Michael O. Garvey, "Death in Terre Haute: The Execution of Timothy McVeigh," *Commonweal*, July 13, 2001, p. 9.

Peter Grier, "Oklahoma City Bombing: Is History Repeating Itself Today?" *Christian Science Monitor*, April 19, 2010, www.csmonitor.com.

Alex Heard, "The Road to Oklahoma City," *New Republic*, vol. 212, May 15, 1995, pp. 15–20.

Michael Hedges, "Letter's Impact Debated; McVeigh's Missive No Help for Appeal," *Houston Chronicle*, May 16, 2001, section A, p.1.

Mark Kindschuh, "Back from the Void (Oklahoma City Search and Rescue Team)," *New Yorker*, vol. 71, no. 12, May 12, 1995, pp. 35–36.

Tracey McVeigh, "Dead Man Talking," *Observer*, April 22, 2001.

Ruaridh Nicoll, "Third Man Lurks in Oklahoma Shadows: Two Bombing Suspects Are in the Dock, but the FBI's Case and Defense Talk of a Conspiracy Rest on the One Who Got Away," *Observer*, December 17, 1995, p. 21.

Antonia Sunderland and Kelsey Menehan, "University Mental Health Clinicians Treat Oklahoma Bombing Victims, Become

Experts on Treating Terror Victims," Robert Wood Johnson Foundation Publications and Research, June 2007, www.rwjf.org.

Joe Swickard, "The Life of Terry Nichols," *Seattle Times*, May 11, 1995, http://seattletimes.nwsource.com.

David Thibodeau, "The Truth About Waco," *Salon*, September 9, 1999, www.salon.com.

Evan Thomas, "Inside the Plot," *Newsweek*, vol. 125, no. 23, June 5, 1995, pp. 24–27.

Kenneth R. Timmerman, "Iraq Was Involved in Oklahoma City," *Insight on the News*, vol. 18, no. 17, May 13, 2002, pp. 8–9.

Patricia J. Williams, "No Vengeance, No Justice," *Nation*, vol. 273, no. 1, July 2, 2001, p. 9.

Marc L. Woodward, "First In: Actions of Engine Company 1," *Fire Engineering*, vol. 148, no. 10, October 1995, pp. 38–43.

Websites

Oklahoma City Bombing Trial (law2.umkc.edu/faculty /projects/ftrials/mcveigh/mcveightrial.html). A project of University of Missouri-Kansas City School of Law professor Douglas O. Lindner, this site provides original court documents; testimony transcripts; a chronology of the bombing and subsequent trial of Timothy McVeigh; a report on Timothy McVeigh in Waco, Texas; and an abundance of other valuable information for students.

Oklahoma City National Museum and Memorial (www .oklahomacitynationalmemorial.org). This website includes details about the Oklahoma City National Museum and Memorial located on the site of the bombing. Students will find video interviews with survivors, articles, a history of the bombing, and photographs, among other items.

Washington Post Special Reports: Oklahoma City Bombing (www.washingtonpost.com/wp-dyn/nation/specials /aroundthenation/okbomb) The *Washington Post*'s Oklahoma City bombing website includes an overview of the events; a photo gallery; a timeline; a large collection of relevant news articles; full-text, step-by-step accounts of McVeigh's trial; and transcripts of interviews with survivors.

INDEX